"*God Breathes on Blended Families* (second edition) is fueled by the experience and passion Moe and Paige have for Blended Families. You will find practical insights and tools that will assist those that find themselves in a Blended Family and for those that are called to serve in marriage and family ministry. *God Breathes on Blended Families* addresses a pressing cultural need. We recommend that everyone in ministry read this book and expand their vision for non-traditional couples and families."

**Eric and Jennifer Garcia**
*Co-Founders, Association of Marriage and Family Ministries, Inc (AMFM)*

"*God Breathes on Blended Families* (second edition) brings hope and practical advice that every parent in a Blended Family should read. The struggles of Blended Families are met with real solutions from the Becnels, who know their Bible and understand the challenges these families face. I am amazed at the practical Biblical approach. This book is a must read for every blended family."

**Dr. Scott Turansky**
*National Center for Biblical Parenting*

"Moe and Paige Becnel and their family are willing to share their trials and victories so that others can grow to understand that God does breathe on Blended Families. This is not just a theory book, but an inside look at a Blended Family that shows people that Blended Families can become a strong family. Thanks, Becnels, for your honesty and example!"

**Dr. Shane Stutzman**
*Lead Pastor, Eastside Baptist Church, Orlando Florida*
*President, Doing Whatever It Takes Ministries*
*Author,* Does Your Church Connect With Blended Families?

"Paige and Moe speak from personal experience but unlike many other authors, they continually take the reader to the Word of God. They encourage everyone to get clarification from God's Word before trying to address whatever problem is at hand at the moment. And like their experience validates, problems with bringing two families together is an everyday event. This book is an encouragement to those wanting to succeed at combining families and lifestyles under one roof."

**Linda Ranson Jacobs**
*Executive Director, DivorceCare for Kids (DC4K)*

# God Breathes on Blended Families

*Second Edition*

# God Breathes on Blended Families

twelve fundamentals to build your family

12

Moe & Paige Becnel

*God Breathes on Blended Families: Twelve fundamentals to build your family* (second edition)
by Moe and Paige Becnel

ISBN: 978-0-9841109-0-2


Library of Congress Cataloging-in-Publication Data



Design and production: Vision Communications Creative and Publishing Services, Inc.

Published by Blending A Family Ministry

Printed in the United States of America

*Dedicated with all our love to all of our children*

Melanie Becnel Broga
Jonathan Broga
Nicole Morriz Duplechain
Brad Duplechain
Jordan Becnel
Kristin Nealy Becnel
Kristen Morriz Young
Jessica Becnel Schleigh
Lance Schleigh

# Table of Contents

# Foreword

IT IS WITH A HUMBLE HEART I write this foreword along with my precious wife. When I was approached by the Becnels for this task, it was truly an honor. Moe and Paige have not only been mentors, but an inspiration in our marriage. I remember when Moe gave me the copy of *God Breathes on Blended Families* (first edition), my then fiancé and I went through the book hanging on to each word, every sentence as if it were *fine gold*. It proved to be more precious than gold, because the treasures we found within those pages were more valuable than gold. Our marriage is not perfect, but the joy we share in our home with our children is now, nevertheless, outstanding.

We were truly blessed while dating to have the Becnels not only as our singles pastors and mentors, but also as our friends. Like many Blended Families, we struggled with challenges such as "You're not my Dad," and other similar issues. I remember the night we told our children we were getting married; all three started crying because they did not want their mother to marry me. I was devastated, but Moe pulled me aside and reminded me that children are hurting too during the divorce, and their mother marrying another person ends their previous family, so more times than not, it will be met with great resistance. Patience and love will win out in the end.

I remember having dinner at Ana's house one evening prior to our marriage when my soon-to-be "new daughter" asked me, "Shouldn't you go home? Your mother is probably worried about you," (I was 35 at the time). Now we all laugh about those times, but at the time it was a struggle and heart breaking. All three of our children are from my wife's previous marriage; I had none, but now, I love these three more than I could ever love my own. You see, they were not born to me, I chose those children, and they are now my children. (At least when they mess up, my wife calls them "my children.")

During the gold rush, a miner did not just walk into the mountains and start grabbing nuggets off the ground. They had to dig, they had to labor; many times for years with sometimes no fruit of their labor. When many did not see immediate results, they quit, (see where I am going), but those who persisted would start finding a nugget here, a nugget there, sometimes few and far-between. Very few miners made a strike by accident quickly. If you want to find the gold in your Blended Family, it will take a lot of hard work, but persistence is the key.

Tough times, like those before the wedding and especially after, are what increase the divorce rate significantly among Blended Families versus first time marriages. This is why I implore you to not only read this book, but to study it along with the Word of God before blending your family. If you have already blended, it is not too late; read and study this book along with seeking not only godly counsel, but godly mentors to be there when these trials arise, because, they will arise. How well you and your spouse respond to the trials will determine how well your family blends.

Grace and peace,
Patrick and Ana Sharp | Willis, Texas
Blended Family October 13, 2000

# Introduction

ON JULY 1, 1997, we celebrated our eighth wedding anniversary. As an anniversary surprise, our five children presented us with a video they had spent more than two months producing.

Titled "The Becnel Bunch," the video began with a takeoff on *The Brady Bunch*, complete with our children singing their own version of the familiar TV theme song. The video continued with photographs and clips of each family member, including our Labrador retriever, Chloe, as well as images from family vacations, birthday parties, and other family memories.

The highlight of the video, however, was a series of comments written by our children about each other and about our family. Here are some of their comments:

> "Jordan is definitely the person to hang around if you're in a bad mood. He will make you smile over the stupidest things. He has a love for people and a joy for life that I admire."
>
> "Jessica looks up to me and makes me feel important."
>
> "Paige is my best friend. She's a blast to be around and has the true heart of a servant—a clean servant."
>
> "I'm proud to have Moe as my dad. He stands behind us no matter how crazy our ideas are. He brings our family together."

"Our family is now one. It's a big, exciting, funny family."

"We are one. We have grown together through the years."

At the end of the video, our children wrote in:

Thanks for the laughs,
Thanks for the tears,
Thanks for the last eight years.
We love you!

## A Celebration

The video blew us away. After eight long years our children were declaring—and finally feeling—that the seven of us were a family. As we sat back digesting the content and meaning of the video, we realized two important things.

First, we realized that the video was a celebration—not just of our eighth anniversary—but a celebration that our family had experienced a transformation. We were now becoming what we had hoped our new family would be.

Second, our children had seen a change in our family—in how our relationships had grown.

Our children wanted to celebrate the changes they were experiencing. Children need a thriving family atmosphere; anything less will breed instability and insecurity in their lives. The video demonstrated that it was important to our children that we had become a family unit. This realization was, to them, significant enough to justify investing eight weeks of their time into collecting photos, preparing scripts and songs, and locating the equipment they needed to make a video to honor and celebrate our Blended Family.

## A Long Journey

On that eighth anniversary we commemorated not only eight years of matrimony, but also how far we had all come since July 1, 1989, when our marriage united not only the two of us, but also our children [Paige's two daughters and Moe's two daughters and one son]. On our wedding day, we began experiencing the numerous struggles involved in making two separate households a united family.

To our disappointment, moving from a stepfamily to a family did not happen quickly. Instead, the seven of us found ourselves living with the arguments, frustrations, disappointments, disrespect, resentment, and day-to-day turmoil experienced by most young Blended Families. Our new life together included issues of children versus stepchildren, new rules and whose rules, competition for time, attention and affection, new schools, losing old friends and making new friends—again.

During the first few years there were isolated moments of closeness, but no sustained unity or harmony. There were many times when we wondered if we would ever overcome functioning as a fragmented unit and move on to becoming a family.

But much to our joy, it did happen. After years of work and prayer, our fractured family was at last made whole. Our children finally came to enjoy being part of our family, and each member began to appreciate and enjoy the others.

## Sustained Unity

Do families really blend? We have heard from professionals who say that stepfamilies do not and will not blend. They believe remarriages with children will, at best, only cope with the issues.

When we married in 1989, there were no godly resources for Blended

Families. At that time psychologists, most of whom had no personal experience with Blended Families, were only able to offer their clients coping techniques. A common phrase, which we heard all-too-often, was "blenders have blades."

We believed God for more where our family was concerned and diligently sought Him for His ways. The result is that our gracious Father God did an amazing work in our family.

Our children ranged from age two years to sixteen years when we married, and ages ten to twenty-four when they produced The Becnel Bunch video in 1997. In 2005, a licensed therapist asked us what each of our adult children would say about the family "today." We thought that was a fair question since we have purposed not to give false hope through Blending A Family Ministry, so we asked them. Following are our children's responses in their own words:

**Melanie:** "To Mom, Dad, Jordan, Kristin, Nicole, Brad, Kristen, Charles and Jessica—I love our family! Although we don't get to see each other often since we're so spread out over the states, when we do, it seems no time has passed, and we just pick right up where we left off. I love that all my siblings (and parents) are godly inspirations to me. We are so blessed to have a family that loves each other unconditionally despite our imperfections. We are closer than most biological families that I know!"

**Nicole:** "I could not imagine my life without Dad (Moe), Melanie, Jordan, and Jessica in it."

**Jordan:** "I would definitely say that our family is truly what God would say a family is by His Word. Now, we are not even close to being 'the Cleavers.' I am saying that without God we would be like most other blended families. He is the one true reason we are the way we are. I know that if something would ever happen to anyone, no matter if step or half, I know we would all come together and hold each other up."

**Kristen:** "My family is everything to me. My family is two dads, two moms, three sisters, one brother, two brothers-in-law, one sister-in-law and three nieces. I love them all equally because in my life they have all played an equal part. I cannot imagine my life without any of them. It wouldn't be complete."

**Jessica:** "I think our family has become a whole. We have grown into each other's lives...we function as one. The love and support from each and every one of us shines when we are together."

We are not saying that our family suddenly became, or has since become, perfect. Our family had flaws and continues to have flaws because every human being has flaws. In any family, individual members will have different personalities, different likes, and their own pet peeves. Yet today, as Melanie stated, our family members are closer than many biological families we know.

And although blending a family did require our time, effort, perseverance, and patience, we can take no credit for the transformation that took place within us. Instead, we recognize our united family as God's supernatural provision. God has done awesome things in our family. We are amazed at the restoration He created in our lives and our children's lives after divorce. God promises His blessings to those who serve Him and seek His face. The condition of our family is proof of those blessings.

And our family continues to grow. In 2009, four children are married and we have six grandchildren.

After all they have been through as children who experienced divorce, today our children love God and are serving Him in many different ways.

Melanie is a small group leader and leads classes in the children's ministry at Dulles Community Church (DCC) in South Riding, Virginia. Her husband, Jonathan, leads worship for Echo, DCC's youth ministry, and performs in the DCC FX Family Experience drama productions.

Nicole and her husband, Brad, are active members of Healing Place Church in Baton Rouge, Louisiana, where Brad is employed as the church's communications director. Nicole volunteers in the women's ministry.

Jordan is the Worship & Creative Arts Pastor at Bayside Community Church in Bradenton, Florida, and his wife, Kristin, is the creative director there as well.

Kristen and her husband, Charles, were missionaries in Swaziland, Africa, for one and one-half years serving aids orphans, and are currently the youth pastors at Bayside Community Church in Bradenton, Florida.

Jessica is presently in college.

We only boast of our children to give God glory and to show how God has healed their hearts of hurts they did not deserve and has turned their lives around—toward Him.

We wrote this book to bring encouragement, hope, and help to other

Blended Families who are struggling, and who truly want to become a solid, loving family. We encourage you to take comfort, knowing there is a Light that, when invited in, will pierce any and every darkness. That Light is Jesus, the Light of the World and the Light of Life.

> *. . . the same Lord is Lord of all and richly blesses all who call on Him, for everyone who calls on the name of the Lord will be saved* (Romans 10: 12–13).

The same Lord who united our family wants to help your family. What He has done for the Becnels, He will do for you! —*Moe and Paige*

# Twelve Fundamentals to Build Your Family

AS YOU PROCEED through this book, you will discover twelve truths (fundamentals) that when applied will shape your Blended Family into a loving family.

1. God is all-knowing, even about Blended Families (Chapter 2).

2. A strong marriage becomes the foundation of your strong family (Chapter 3).

3. Understand that you have an adversary who is at work to undermine your family (Chapter 4).

4. It is vital to build relationships with the children (Chapter 4 and throughout book).

5. Establish one set of rules and discipline for everyone in your home (Chapter 4).

6. Learn and apply God's order for your family (Chapters 4 and 5).

7. Achieve individual wholeness, because who you are dictates what you are able to bring into a marriage and family (Chapter 5).

8. Understand and help the children in your family heal and connect (Chapter 6, and throughout book).

9. A stepparent has many responsibilities (Chapter 7).

10. Guard your family from external hurts (Chapter 8).

11. Establish family goals (Chapter 9).

12. Understand and utilize the power of prayer (Chapter 10).

# Definitions

THE FOLLOWING WORDS and terms are defined according to their intended use in this publication:

| | |
|---|---|
| *Blended Family* | Any marriage in which at least one spouse becomes a stepparent (new parent), regardless of the age of the children. (The term is treated as a proper name in this book.) |
| *blend* | To mix together, especially in such a way as to form one product: to mix together, so that the things mixed cannot be separated or individually distinguished. |
| *biological parent* | The maternal or paternal parent. |
| *extended family* | The parents, brothers, sisters, grandparents, aunts, uncles, former spouses, former in-laws, and friends of both spouses. |
| *former spouse* | More commonly referred to as "ex-spouse" or "ex." |
| *new child* | A child gained through marriage; your spouse's biological child; stepchild. |
| *new parent* | The spouse who gains a child or children through marriage or adoption; stepparent. |

## Chapter 1

# Restoration After Death or Divorce

*In 1994 our family moved to Baton Rouge, Louisiana. The home we bought had no kitchen pantry, so Moe and I went to an antique auction to find a large piece of furniture to serve that purpose. We found an armoire we liked but could not get to it to inspect it. As the auction went on, the furniture pieces in front of it were auctioned off and then the workers began to stack sold furniture in front of it.*

*Moe spoke to an employee about the armoire, and he said no one had shown interest in it in the last six weeks. He asked Moe, "Do you want to bid on it?" We did, and we won the bid at $365.00 without inspecting it.*

*Moe picked up the armoire two days later, and it began to fall apart in our trailer on the way home. We were so frustrated. We reassembled it in the house and built shelves in it. A few weeks later when a furniture repairman came to fix a bed, he saw the armoire. We told him the story. He began to educate us, informing us that it was a French traveling armoire designed for college students moving into a dormitory; it was built to come apart and be put back together. He inspected it and found a signature on the bottom. He quickly appraised the armoire at $10,000.00.*

*In the life of this armoire, someone had lost sight of its value. When our lives have fallen apart, we often fail to see the value in ourselves that God has never lost sight of. Father God has a heart to redeem, revive and restore us.* —Paige

▪ ▪ ▪

SPOUSES IN BLENDED FAMILIES may have come from a variety of circumstances; some have experienced either the death of a spouse or divorce, others may have been a single parent who was not previously married, while for others the Blended Family may be their first marriage.

Before we begin discussing Blended Family issues, let us first address the issue of divorce and God's forgiveness.

God's Word, the Holy Bible, is quite clear that divorce is to be avoided if at all possible.

*I [God] hate divorce* (Malachi 2:16).

It is God's plan for relationships to last a lifetime, particularly marriage relationships that are to mirror the relationship God has with His Church—you and I.

Divorce is the death of a marriage relationship. If the marriage produced children, then that family was a small civilization. Just as cancer deteriorates the physical body and ends human life, divorce is the outcome of a combination of various offenses and unforgiveness, which ultimately results in the death of a marriage and the fall of a civilization.

Offenses that lead to relationship failure include selfishness, pride, arrogance, disrespect, adultery and other forms of infidelity, anger, violence, physical abuse, verbal abuse, criticism, sarcasm, neglect of a spouse, neglect of the marriage covenant, lack of commitment to each other, and a quitting mentality. There are others.

We have heard people attempt to validate or justify their divorce by saying, "It is God's will" or "God allowed it." In very rare instances is divorce the will of God. Divorce is ultimately man's decision and man's choice, not God's choice.

The negative impact of divorce creates a ripple effect reaching far beyond the husband and wife. Many other people are emotionally wounded by each and every divorce—especially the children involved and close extended family members. Even close friends disappear because they do not want to be "caught in the middle" or forced to take sides.

As two people who have both experienced divorce, we can certainly understand why God hates divorce; it is painful for all involved. It rips people apart and causes deep hurts that take a long time—with the help of God—to heal. Divorce dramatically changes people's lives, including those of the extended family members, and alters plans for many years into the future. Most children continue to reprocess the pain of loss every three to five years—and for years to come. Many adult children continue to struggle with biological parents who do not get along, ending up playing referee between bitter parents and planning their holidays among multiple families.

## God's Forgiveness

There are some people and organizations who believe all past divorce is sin, and continues to be a sin in one's present life. They think people are permanently "stained" by divorce, that God does not forgive divorce, that neither God nor the Christian Church have use for divorced people, and that God will not bless remarriages or Blended Families.

Such belief pre-judges the wife who was being physically beaten by her husband, or the woman who ended the marriage because the father was sexually abusing the children in the home. This belief system does not take into consideration repeated infidelity in the marriage or other unacceptable behavior, and it discounts God's mercy and grace, which have been freely given to all.

These ideas imply that divorced people are not as good as those who have never experienced divorce, and that divorced people are neither worthy of, nor entitled to, the forgiveness and abundant life Jesus came to give us. This attitude by society, acquaintances, and family causes some divorced people to walk with low levels of hope that result in low expectations for their future and the future of their children.

We have met remarried men and women who still carry a sense of failure and guilt because of their divorce, and who are hesitant to "admit" they are now in a Blended Family. They lack faith in the grace offered by Jesus Christ, or struggle to believe that the full life Jesus offers in John 10:10 is for them.

## True Repentance

Nowhere in the Bible do we find that God wants His children (those who accept Christ as their Savior and Lord) to live unforgiven and defeated. Instead, the Bible teaches that God is a God of restoration. When there is true repentance from our sins (stopping our offensive behavior and unforgiveness toward God and others), God is gracious to redeem us and bring forth complete restoration in our lives.

Scripture has much to say concerning the forgiveness of *all* sin, which is available to each person through Christ Jesus. This forgiveness includes forgiveness of those sins leading to divorce.

In John Chapter 4, Jesus met the woman at the well who had been divorced five times and was now with another man. Jesus did not call her a sinner or verbally beat her up about her life of sin; He always met people where they were in life. Jesus directed her to the Living Waters available through Him so she would never thirst again. She believed in Jesus and immediately became an evangelist for Him by telling all the people of her town to come meet the Christ. Many believed in Jesus and were added to the Kingdom of God that day.

Did she deserve this favorable treatment? No. None of us deserve God's grace and God's forgiveness for any of *our* sin, yet Jesus laid His life down to forgive our sins; yours, mine . . . everyone's.

The following Bible verses speak of God's love, mercy, grace, and forgiveness:

> *If we confess our sins, He is faithful and just and will forgive us our sins and purify us from all unrighteousness* (1 John 1:9).

> *He forgives all my sins and heals all my diseases; He redeems my life from the pit and crowns me with love and compassion* (Psalm 103:4).

> *. . . as far as the east is from the west, so far has He removed our transgressions from us* (Psalm 103:12).

> *. . . it [love] keeps no record of wrongs* (1 Corinthians 13:5).

> *The thief comes only to steal and kill and destroy; I [Jesus] have come that they may have life, and have it to the full* (John 10:10).

## Repentance Defined

*Repent* is defined as "such sorrow for past life as produces a new life."

The story of the adulteress in John 8:1–11 is a powerful display of God's love and grace on our lives. Jewish leaders brought a woman who had been caught in the act of adultery to Jesus. In Mosaic Law, people who committed adultery were to be stoned to death. That is what this woman expected as the men who brought her to Jesus came with stones in their hands. It was a dark day for that woman . . . until Jesus came to her aid.

When Jesus forgave the adulteress, He commanded her to "go and sin no more." Jesus forgave her completely, and gave her a second chance to live a new life.

When people divorce because of sins of selfishness, pride, immorality, arrogance, unforgiveness and such, God expects repentance before He forgives and dispenses His grace. If there is no repentance, there is no change in the person's heart, and so God's grace becomes trampled upon. For an individual who has not remarried after divorce, repentance may include asking God if the former marriage should be given another chance to reconcile.

Repentance for remarried couples might include:

- making the commitment to remain faithful to their vows,
- making God the center of their home,
- learning to love and value each other enough to forgive *all* future offenses,
- devoting themselves to the remarriage as "the marriage that *will* last a lifetime," and
- never considering divorce as an option for solving new marriage and family issues.

Remember, God hates divorce (see Malachi 2:16).

When there is true repentance (such sorrow for past life as produces a new life), God forgives completely. The slate is clean. There is no stain. We are as "white as snow" (see Psalm 51:7; Isaiah 1:18).

If you have experienced divorce, know that God wants to restore you. He loves and cherishes you. In your prayer time, ask the Holy Spirit to show you what you did wrong that caused your previous relationships to fail. Ask God to forgive you for the part you played in your previously failed marriage and other relationships. Learn from those mistakes, and vow to God to not repeat them.

## Forgiving Yourself

You must now forgive yourself. It is not God's plan for you to walk in guilt; doing so will prevent you from providing the godly and effective parental leadership your children need in order to grow into healthy and successful adults.

Over the twelve years that we led a single parent ministry at our church, we saw first-hand the effect that walking in guilt had on some single parents. They failed to provide structure, rules and discipline in their children's lives, allowing them to "run wild." We watched some of these children grow up with behavioral problems, and a few became juvenile delinquents. Some of these children had no direction in life when they got older. Some parents continued to financially support their children into their late twenties and thirties . . . well past higher-education years.

Oftentimes, the reason parents behaved this way was because they were walking in guilt. The parent felt guilty that their child was put through divorce, or the other parent died, or the other parent mistreated the child or abandoned them, or the child had to grow up in a single-parent home. So they compensated by giving "bad" gifts such as displays of favoritism, no boundaries, no discipline when rules are not followed, and being the kind of support that hindered the children from growing and maturing to support themselves—gifts that would hurt the children for the rest of their lives.

We see the same guilt behavior carried into Blended Families. Examples of such behavior include:

- not applying rules and discipline,
- not expecting the child/children to become part of the new family,
- allowing the child/children to disrespect the new people in their lives,
- not giving the child/children any responsibility in the new family,
- not requiring minor children to participate in family activities,
- giving gifts to one's own children but not to the spouse's children, and
- allowing children to decide if they "want" to go to church.

Since guilt is so destructive to self, to children, and to the future of a new Blended Family, we *must* learn to walk in the freedom of self-forgiveness and receive the abundant life that Jesus Christ came to give us.

Forgiving yourself is a critical step in completing the forgiveness in your life.

## Faith of a Child

The Bible tells us,

> *Then Jesus called a little child to Him, set him in the midst of them, and said, "Assuredly, I say to you, unless you are converted and become as little children, you will by no means enter the kingdom of heaven. Therefore whoever humbles himself as this little child is the greatest in the kingdom of heaven"* (Matthew 18:2–4).

How do little children behave? They believe their parents, simply trusting what their parents tell them without analysis. Our own children leap into our arms, knowing we will catch them. They cuddle next to us knowing we will cuddle back and not harm them. Jesus is telling adults to have the faith of a child and believe Him—to trust Father God.

As adults, we sometimes have difficulty believing in what we cannot see. Some of us may continue to doubt until we have proof, wanting to see, feel, touch, smell or taste before we believe. Many have discounted God's blessings by calling them "luck" or claiming personal achievement. When circumstances overwhelm us, we often begin to doubt that God even hears our prayers, and doubt even more that prayers will be answered.

The movie *Polar Express* is the story of a boy who doubts there is a real Santa. He is awakened in the night by the arrival of a mystical train that takes him on a ride of discovery. He is skeptical about what is happening, believing he is dreaming, and he doubts the other children who do believe. As the train continues on its journey to the North Pole, the children discover that one of its cars is filled with broken toys, including an Ebenezer Scrooge puppet that tells the boy, "You are a doubter; you don't believe! You are a doubter; you don't believe!"

When the train arrives at the North Pole and the children first see Santa's reindeer leaping with anticipation as they are hitched to the sleigh, the boy cannot hear the bells on the reindeer harnesses because of his doubt. Just as doubt kept the boy in the *Polar Express* story from hearing the sound of bells, our doubt can prevent us from hearing God's voice and receiving all that He has provided for us.

*How do we destroy doubt and increase our faith? How do we become believers—true, complete, uncompromised believers?*

1. Realize that Jesus is the source of your faith, which is given by God.

   *Let us fix our eyes on Jesus, the author and perfecter of our faith* (Hebrews 12:2).

   *Do not think of yourself more highly than you ought, but rather think of yourself with sober judgment, in accordance with the measure of faith God has given you* (Romans 12:3).

2. Read and study God's Word. What you meditate on, you multiply.

   *Consequently, faith comes from hearing the message, and the message is heard through the word of Christ* (Romans 10:17).

3. Surround yourself with believers in God's power. You will become like the company you keep. In 2 Timothy 3:1–5, the Apostle Paul instructs Timothy to beware of unbelievers. Paul said there will be those who have a form of godliness but deny its power. He encouraged Timothy to have nothing to do with them.

   Disconnect from doubters who deny God's power, saying He cannot, or will not, work supernaturally in your life and family.

4. Pray—ask Father God to increase your faith.

*Lord I believe. Help my unbelief!* (Mark 9:24).

At the end of *Polar Express* the boy could hear the reindeer bell ring because be became a believer. So, the question is not, "*What* are you believing for?" Rather, the question is, "*Who* do you believe in?"

The content of this book and the success of our family and yours is based on these three primary biblical truths:

- God's Word is a manual of life filled with God's principles for successful, abundant life. The application of His truth sets us free.
- There is supernatural help available to us. God loves us, and is for us. Once we have applied these principles in our life, God's power shows up to create the life that we cannot attain by ourselves.
- As illustrated throughout the Bible, man has to first follow God's instruction, and then God does His part. Do your part, and God will breathe His breath of life on your marriage and family.

## What Blending A Family Ministry Promotes

No one reading this material should conclude that the authors or the content of this book advocate divorce. Divorce is not acceptable to God, to this ministry, or to us. God's plan is for every marriage to last a lifetime.

*Let your fountain be blessed, and rejoice with the wife of your youth* (Proverbs 5:18).

We both wish we had never experienced divorce. It would have spared us, and many others—including our children, friends and extended family members—a great deal of pain, loss and turmoil. Yet, we know that people make mistakes, and the premise of God's grace is that God meets people where they are in life. Consider the Bible examples of Moses who escaped to the desert after committing murder, the woman at the well who had been married five times, the adulteress who was brought before Jesus to be condemned and stoned, or Paul (Saul) who was defaming Christ and persecuting Christians.

Today the list of people who need to experience God's grace is endless. It includes everyone who needs a savior as well as those who have made mistakes because they did not obey God, and now wish they would have done things differently. God's goal for those mentioned in the Bible was to show His unconditional love to each of them, extend His grace, and change their hearts. Today, God's goal is the same for each of us.

## Our Prayer for You

Father, we pray for every person that reads this book. Help them to find restoration in You as they repent and receive Your forgiveness and grace. Increase their trust in You. Give them the eyes of the Holy Spirit to see what You want them to see, the mind of the Holy Spirit to understand, and a heart of compassion to see their new family as You see them. In Jesus' awesome name. Amen.

## Funny Family Moments

One summer day we took the children fishing in our boat near the Gulf of Mexico. Jordan was lying on the front deck of the boat when a porpoise surfaced about forty yards away. We slowed down and stopped the engine so we could watch the porpoise. Jordan started to make porpoise sounds with his mouth, and Mom (Paige) said, "Hey guys, listen to the porpoise talking to us." Then Jordan chimed up and said, "Mom, that was me." Mom said, "Oops," and we all started laughing.

## Chapter 2

# God's Plan for Blended Families

*Paige Becnel*

*As a child growing up in the Northeast, I can remember bitter cold mornings when I watched the snow fall through our frosted dining room windows. My dad would tell my brother, sister and I, "Don't touch the windows." Most window glass back in that day was not tempered to handle both extreme cold and the touch of a warm human hand at the same time. It would shatter on contact and many times cut the flesh if a person wanted to try defying the physics of it all.*

*Twenty-something years later I found myself looking out of a glass storm door on a gray, colder-than-normal morning. I was now separated, raising two young girls and feeling very alone. Life had not turned out like I thought it would, and as I stood at that door looking out into a sunless sky, I wondered, "If I touch this glass, will it shatter just like my life has? Is there hope in the cold?"* —Paige

▪ ▪ ▪

I CAN ONLY BEGIN by saying that Moe is a wonderful husband and we have a great family.

Our wedding day was fun and full of children—five between the two of us. The four girls were dressed so beautifully, and the lone boy, Jordan, was quite handsome. Thinking of that day brings to mind images of rose petals and daisies, ribbons and white lace, the perfect music, family and friends, and the loving bride and groom. It was perfect.

After the ceremony, Moe and I flew to Los Angeles for our honeymoon, where we enjoyed seven blissful days together. We arrived back home late on a Friday night. I'll never forget the joy of opening the door to find four of our five children asleep on the floor. Hanging above them on the balcony was a huge, hand-lettered banner that said, "Welcome Home Mom and Dad!"

But all too soon, the honeymoon was literally over. Real life set in, and along with it, conflict. I did not like the way Moe corrected my children and he did not like the way I corrected his. My daughters came to me with pitiful faces full of hurt, telling me what "he" said they could or could not do. The rules I had established in my former home were suddenly challenged by the rules Moe had established, and vice versa.

"You don't discipline your children enough!"

"Why don't your children listen when I correct them?"

"My children are not allowed to do that!"

"Well, my children are!"

I thought he was wrong. He thought I was wrong. There were not many things we agreed on, yet we did agree that we did not want another divorce, and that God would make a way. We dealt with the same issues repeatedly, day after day, month after month, with no resolution. It was a never-ending cycle. As time went by Moe and I began to resent each other. Each set of children began to resent their new parent.

What had happened to our perfect family?

## Struggles of Blended Families

I prayed fervently every day for our new family. Even through the hard times when Moe and I did not see eye-to-eye, I always spent time with God, interceding for every member of our family. God, I thought, would surely honor those prayers.

And He did. But not the way I thought He would.

During the early years of our marriage, I wondered if our house would ever feel like a warm, loving home. I felt a dark cloud was hanging over Moe and me. Just when I thought we were making progress in an area of our marriage or in relationships within our family, something would break loose and blindside us.

Moe and I never seemed to agree on anything when a decision had to be made concerning the children. The same statement was present in every conversation. "If you would do this, then I would do that." We never really solved anything; we only walked away from our discussions confused and hurt by each other.

I became more and more frustrated, and remember saying more than once, "Why even try to talk about it? We never solve anything anyway."

I sometimes felt I prayed in circles. I would search the scriptures for answers and find reassurance. God would sustain me in His joy and praise. But then I would find myself facing the same wall I thought I had already climbed. Was God even listening to me in my prayer time? Did He see us flailing about, trying to make something of all this?

During this time, I happened to see a television documentary on Blended Families. The program featured interviews with members of Blended Families, and discussed the struggles they were facing. But then, something was said that really caught my attention. A psychologist stated that it takes a Blended Family an average of four to eight years to "gel," and finally feel like a family.

I literally stopped what I was doing. I remember thinking to myself, "That may be true for some families, but we live and breathe for God. Doesn't the Scripture say that nothing is impossible with God (see Luke 1:37)?" The rest of the world may have to wait four to eight years, but I did not think that would be necessary for our family.

"God," I prayed, "Did You hear that? Four to eight years to gel? You are bigger than that. With You on our side, we will become a loving family in less time than that!"

Looking back, I'm glad I didn't know what was ahead because it took the Becnel/Morriz family seven years to mesh, melt together, and become the family that our children eventually celebrated.

But even though it took longer than I had hoped, God was always, and still is, in control. He heard my prayers loud and clear—a lot clearer than I ever thought He did.

## God's Knowledge of Blended Families

God knows us much better than we give Him credit for. After all, He created us, and created us for a purpose.

> *Before I formed you in the womb I knew you* (Jeremiah 1:5).

> *"For I know the plans I have for you," declares the Lord, "plans to prosper you and not harm you, plans to give you a hope and a future"* (Jeremiah 29:11).

One day when I was in prayer, I questioned God as to His knowledge of a Blended Family. Can you imagine questioning God? It sounds so disrespectful, but God has a way of extending His grace abundantly to our lives over and over again.

I sat quietly, listening for that still, small voice that comes from deep within the soul and ministers to the heart. Then I heard in my thoughts, "My Son was a stepchild, and part of a Blended Family."

That statement startled me. I reread the story in Matthew Chapter 1 of Jesus' conception, Joseph and Mary's quiet marriage, and Jesus' birth. How many times I had read this passage, yet had never before seen that Joseph was Jesus' stepfather. What an awesome task God had given to Joseph, a simple carpenter—to raise the Son of God. The very breath of God was in their family.

## God Has a Plan

But God did not stop there when He spoke to me that day. Instead, He went on to reveal a most precious lesson about our family through the creation story.

> *In the beginning God created the heavens and the earth. Now the earth was formless and empty, darkness was over the surface of the deep, and the Spirit of God was hovering over the waters* (Genesis 1:1–2).

This was exactly how I was feeling and seeing our family—empty, formless, and definitely dark. God had certainly nailed that one!

I was also intrigued by the use of the word "hovering" in this verse. "Helicopters hover," I thought. Before they land on a designated spot, they hover close, looking and preparing, then finally land to perform the mission they were sent to do.

In the Greek language, the word *hover* means, "to brood over." Webster defines *brood* as "to cherish, to love, or to hold dear." Now this was stirring my spirit. "How," I thought, "could God cherish a dark, formless, empty, nothing?" And then the still, small voice answered me, saying, "I see potential in nothing."

What a powerful revelation! God sees potential in darkness, in emptiness, and in nothingness. Why? Because it is a place in which His grace and power can create something beautiful.

The darkness and emptiness in our family was not a threat to God. On the contrary, it was a chance, an opportunity, for Him to breathe upon us and work a miracle. God was hovering over our family, looking for the perfect spot to begin His mission. And He found it, right in the middle of our hearts.

The creation story goes on to say,

> *And God said, "Let there be light," and there was light. God saw that the light was good and He separated the light from the darkness* (Genesis 1: 3–4).

God's first act of creation was to create light, and to separate the light from the darkness.

In our case, God had to separate the light from the darkness in our lives. There were many dark, void spots in our family, which I believe are present in most Blended Families. What are some of these dark areas?

- We keep walls up so we will not get hurt again, which prevents the marriage and family from growing.
- There is little or no bonding between us and our spouse's children.
- We are sterner, less patient, and less tolerant with our spouse's children than with our own.
- We do not love our spouse's children as we love our own.

- Our new children do not respect our authority, nor do they respect the new family.

If you see some of these or other dark areas in your own life, don't worry. God has a plan. And He will reveal it to you in His time—possibly through the course of your reading this book.

## God's Timing

When I heard the psychologist say that it usually took a Blended Family four to eight years to gel, I was sure that God would work on our family much faster than that. After all, He is God. He has everything under His control.

Eight years later I asked God why it had taken so long for us to become one. He again took me back to the creation story. I realized then that God could have created the earth in one day—one moment—one second. Instead, He invested six days, completing everything according to His plan, in His timing.

What was His strategy? The answer lies in Genesis 1:3–19. God spent four days separating the light from the dark, the sky from the expanse below, the seas from the landmasses, and the evening from the morning. He created fleshly life on the fifth day, mankind on the sixth, and He rested on the seventh. God spent four days separating and getting things in order for His ultimate creation—us.

Before He could unite our family, God had a lot of separating to do in Moe and me. He had to separate our thoughts from His will for us, our pride from His humility, and our past from the plan He was trying to bring forth in us now.

## Our Thoughts

Our thoughts can so often get in the way of what God is trying to do for us. We question God with endless "Whys" and "Why nots." We often live life according to our plans and ideas rather than inquiring of God's Word for the wisdom we need in order to make our decisions.

> *As the heavens are higher than the earth, so are My ways higher than your ways, and my thoughts than your thoughts* (Isaiah 55:9).

We must remove all thoughts of doubt about what God can do in our lives and make a way for Him to give us the prosperous future He desires for us.

> *"For I know the plans I have for you," declares the Lord, "plans to prosper you and not to harm you, plans to give you a hope and a future"* (Jeremiah 29:11).

We must first be willing to allow God's plan to reveal itself, then we must be patient. So often, God gives us His plan for our lives, but we doubt His magnificent power because things don't work out easily or move quickly enough to suit us.

The truth is, God would probably work a lot faster, but we get in His way. Have you ever tried cleaning your house with your whole family at home? It's almost impossible. You just finish vacuuming when someone spills crumbs all over the floor. You've just put the mop away when someone comes in the back door with mud on his or her shoes.

More than once, I've watched Moe try to mow the lawn, only to have to stop to move a bike, a water hose, a golf ball, or any one of a dozen items that someone in our family has added to the landscape.

Obstacles like these make work more difficult and time consuming.

But what about God's work in our lives? Do we make it difficult for Him? Do we allow our pride to get in the way of His work on humility? What about taking a left turn when His will is clearly to the right? Has His construction in the area of patience been slowed because we've been stomping our feet, rolling our eyes, and reminding God that we have a time schedule?

Human reasoning usually leads us down the path of failure. Examples of flawed human reasoning are:

- "God is not interested in me because I have not walked in His ways for so many years."
- "God will never bless my re-marriage."
- "My children will be fine. They will bounce back from divorce."
- "It is okay to live together without being married."
- "Our children are getting along great while we are dating. They will be happy if we get married."
- "My spouse's children do not want me in their life."
- "I am not their biological parent, so I am not responsible for them."
- Spouses having separate checkbooks or taking separate vacations with their biological children are considered acceptable ideas.
- "I just avoid my out-of-control teenage stepson."
- "My parents do not accept my new spouse, so I just go by myself to visit them. No big deal."

Our negative thoughts and flawed human reasoning are like muddy shoes, trampling all over the work God has done and is trying to do in our lives. Instead of continuing these thought patterns, we must be patient and give God the time and permission He needs to create a new thing in us. We must step back from the work zone, and let God finish what He has begun.

## Dating or Engaged?

We urge couples that are not yet married to proceed slowly and look for any "red flags" in their relationship, in their children, and in how their partner is interacting with and responding to their children.

We have personally seen children who got along fine while a couple was dating, but then everything changed on or shortly after the wedding day. We will address this issue more thoroughly in Chapter 5.

If you are contemplating a marriage that will result in the blending of a family, now is the time to prepare. I encourage you to read through this book, several times if necessary, in order to prepare yourself and help prepare your children for your future marriage and new family. As you prepare to enter a marriage and a Blended Family with many potential dynamics that can work against it, keep in mind that an ounce of prevention is worth a hundred pounds of cure.

Based on our personal experience and that of working with other Blended Families, we recommend the following:

1. Be sure there is no chance to reconcile with your former spouse. To you it may be a "long shot" or even "impossible," but reconciling is always God's first choice. God will need to heal each of you individually before reconciling is possible. Oftentimes, moving into new relationships too quickly can cloud what God is trying to do in your life.
2. Also, consider the same about the person you are dating. Have they

given God a chance to reconcile their former marriage? You do not want to hinder what God is trying to do in someone else's life.

3. Examine your past relationship failures to determine what part (habits, pet-peeves, negative attitudes, words, actions, negative reactions, etc.) you played in the deterioration of those relationships.
4. If you lost a spouse to death, we strongly suggest you find a grief recovery class so you can jumpstart your healing prior to getting involved in another relationship. If such classes are not available, then read some books on the subject. Even if you are already remarried, it is never too late to seek your healing from past loss.
5. If you have been through divorce, we urge you to attend a divorce recovery program for the same reasons as in number 3 above. The first time Moe and I taught a divorce care program that we had written, the Holy Spirit showed each of us areas of our life in which we still had hurts, anger, unforgiveness, and such. At that time we had been married twelve years. How much better our marriage and family would have been in the early years if we were healed of those things prior to our marriage. Occasionally a married person would attend the class because they were struggling with their previous divorce, or letting go of anger or unforgiveness toward a former spouse. The class helped them greatly.
6. Keep yourself pure before marriage. In God's plan for our life, sexual intimacy is reserved for the marriage bed, and sexual immorality separates you from His presence and His plan. When we cross that line, we make decisions based on emotions rather than God's plan, and we block His blessing on our life. If you have already crossed that line, *stop the behavior immediately!* Repent and start your relationship over in God's way. You will always come out on top when

you honor God in your life. Do not ignore the red flags. Make the necessary adjustments now, even if it means breaking up or separating from the person you are dating or engaged to for a time.

7. Attend a pre-marriage course together, and a marriage seminar. If your partner will not go, go alone.
8. Read other marriage enrichment and parenting books to prepare for your new marriage covenant.

## Our Pride

The biggest area God had to work on in Moe and me was our pride. Our refusal to let go of certain things that seemed so important to each of us—including areas of parental rules and discipline—turned molehills into mountains.

As we have provided guidance to many Blended Families, we see that pride is a huge factor in remarriages. For instance, consider the fact that remarriages are made up mostly of two older adults who were independent and had become seasoned in their ways. Add to this the fact that many spouses entering remarriage were single parents who had become Mom, Dad, financial provider, care-giver, team coach, taxi, tutor, and business administrator—and they did it all alone. Then they marry someone just like them, someone who is just as confident and independent. This can make for a volatile collision as each attempts to hold on to doing things "my way" in the new marriage and family.

*Pride* is defined as "justifiable self-respect, superiority, or arrogance." Pride is all about self; it looks to self without regard of other people's feelings, needs, or desires. Pride will whisper, "You deserve it," or "It's their fault," or "You can quit drinking; have another." Prideful statements, even when made unconsciously, will cause a spouse or children to feel inferior, insignificant, unappreciated, and worthless. Some of the symptoms of pride include:

- a "What's in it for me" attitude (a self-serving attitude),
- the idea that "My opinions or ideas are always better than the other person's idea,"
- things have to be done "My way, or no way,"
- criticism or sarcasm are frequent, followed by "I was only joking,"
- seldom or never admitting to being wrong,
- not being sorry, or finding it difficult to say, "I am sorry,"
- being reluctant or seeing no need to apologize,
- justifying one's actions, especially when wrong,
- comparing self to others (which brings pride or discouragement),
- being unteachable ("Don't tell me how to raise my kids"), and
- unforgiveness.

*Pride only breeds quarrels, but wisdom is found in those who take advice* (Proverbs 13:10).

The Bible gives account of two families that were severely damaged by pride. In Genesis 16 and 21, we find the story of Abraham, Sarah, Hagar, and Ishmael shows how pride led to control, manipulation, and jealousy. The family became divided, and Abraham had to dismiss a wife and son from his home. This is the first recorded divorce that we have found in the Bible.

In Genesis Chapter 27 the story of Jacob and Esau, who were the sons of Isaac, started with competition at birth and continued throughout their life. Jacob stole Esau's legal birthright. Their lives were marked by deception, manipulation, disrespect, and family breakdown.

## Pride and Opinions

Most of us would agree that everyone has an opinion on just about everything. Opinions can cause significant and long-term trouble in relationships. Believe it or not, our own opinions are not always right, and other people's opinions are not always wrong.

Why are our opinions not always right? Opinions are partially based on facts, but they are also based on individual personality, personal preferences, backgrounds, educational experience, family history (things Mom and Dad did or said), religious beliefs, and other factors. The problem with opinions is not that everyone has one, but that each person thinks theirs is right.

Because of the close tie to our individual backgrounds and history, opinions can take on the nature of being part of our "identity." We can put so much value on our own opinions that they can become a stumbling block to us and to our relationships. This is why, when someone does not accept our opinion, we may feel rejected or even get offended. This is also why our spouse or children might feel insignificant and worthless if their opinion or idea is seldom or never valued.

God made us all different on purpose—by His design. We need to embrace this thought and appreciate the differences in others. Instead of attempting to enforce our opinions and ideas as rules over others, we should consider differing opinions and ideas for a change, thereby showing respect to other family members.

For Moe and me, this meant we had to stop the blame-game, blaming each other and the children for the problems in our family, and begin to take personal responsibility for the issues at hand. We also had to stop worshipping our own opinions, and start to value each other's ideas.

God had to take time to teach each of us to sacrifice ourselves instead of expecting more from each other. We each had to become less rigid and more flexible, warmer instead of colder, and give up our ways for His way.

Pride only serves to hurt, separate and destroy. There is no truth in pride. We must choose to lay it aside and let God's humility take charge of our hearts.

## Our Past Baggage

God also had to remind Moe and me over and over again that our past was not a stumbling block for Him. Father God's future for His children is so much greater than we could ever imagine. His will for each of us is positive, powerful, and life-giving, yet if we do not take the time and effort to unload any baggage we are carrying, our new spouse and family will have to carry the weight of this baggage as well. Such baggage may include:

- guilt,
- undisclosed and habitual sin,
- past failures that affect our attitudes and actions today,
- past wounds that still hurt,
- unforgiveness
- a critical spirit,
- anger,
- oppression or depression,
- blaming others for the problems in our own lives,
- disappointments,
- excessive worry,

- doubting God,
- financial debt, and
- other people, such as friends or family members, who drag us down.

At the airport we check our bags so we do not have to carry them during the flight. The airline restricts how much baggage weight can be brought on the plane. The plane has a passenger and freight weight limit that, if exceeded, could cause the plane to crash, especially when experiencing the added stress of turbulence.

The baggage in our lives has the same restriction. The heavy loads that both we, as well as our families, often carry can cause our relationships to crash.

What if there was a place where we could check all of the emotional baggage we have collected and continue to carry throughout our life? Is there a place to check those bags once and for all? There is! We can place them and leave them at the foot of the Cross of Jesus Christ.

Everyone has baggage of some sort; we are all imperfect beings living in an imperfect world. Divorce is never an escape from baggage; it actually creates more baggage. Yet, checking baggage at the Cross frees a person to live the more abundant life that Jesus came to give us.

> *Therefore, if anyone is in Christ, he is a new creation; the old has gone, the new has come* (2 Corinthians 5:17).

> *Cast all your anxiety on Him because He cares for you* (1Peter 5:7).

> *Come to Me all you who are weary and burdened, and I will give you rest* (Matthew 11:28).

Right now, I encourage you to take an inventory of the baggage you may be carrying and make the decision to unload it. For additional help in identifying any baggage you may be carrying, see Appendix B.

## God's Plan

One day God spoke something very special to me. He said, "The biggest dream you have for yourself is my smallest thought for you."

In the beginning, it was only after He had finished separating and putting things in their proper order that God begin to create. He did a perfect job, creating so much with such precision and care. Then, the seventh day was a day of rest.

You and your new family are a part of God's wonderful masterpiece. And once you make God's plan a part of your life, your day of rest is on its way.

> *He will bestow on us a crown of beauty instead of ashes, the oil of gladness instead of mourning, and a garment of praise instead of despair* (Isaiah 61:3).

God loves Blended Families. He hates divorce, but He loves the person who has been through divorce.

> *I will be the God of all the families of Israel, and they will be My people* (Jeremiah 31:1, NKJV).

We believe this scripture refers to not only all the vast numbers of families in His Kingdom, but also includes all the many types of families, as there were the same types of families when that scripture was written as there are now, including biological families, single parent families, Blended Families, widows, orphans, grandparents raising grandchildren, and others.

Do not give up in your efforts to blend your family. You can and will make it. But you cannot accomplish this alone.

> *". . . Not by might nor by power, but by My Spirit," says the Lord Almighty* (Zechariah 4: 6).

The Greek word for *spirit* is the same as the word for *breath*. Allow God's Spirit to take charge of your heart and your home. Allow God to breathe on you.

He will show Himself strong in your family!

## Our Prayer for You

Father God, we pray for the Blended Family reading this book and for all of their needs, which are being brought to You today. We know how close You are to them right now. You never leave them nor forsake them. Show Yourself to them and let them feel Your breath in their lives.

Help them to see the areas where You are trying to make a separation to remove flawed reasoning and show Your thoughts and Your plans, to remove pride and develop a servant heart, and to leave the past baggage and look to the new thing You are doing in their midst. Strengthen them in their journey to bring their family together as one to serve You. We love You and give You all praise and honor.

In Jesus' mighty name. Amen.

## Funny Family Moment

In December of 1996, six of us set out in our Mazda van on a driving vacation to visit Grandma and Grandad (Paige's parents) in Indianapolis. It was very cold (the temperature did not get above twenty-eight degrees for five straight days) and Dad (Moe) was having a difficult time keeping the van windows defrosted. In order to keep the windows free of frost, he ran the air conditioner because running the heater would put him to sleep at the wheel.

The entire trip the family complained, "We're freezing!" Dad reminded them repeatedly, "Get under the blanket and take a nap!" Their response became "Rhear," a term of endearment for Dad.

"Rhear" was heard repeatedly over the following days. Toward the end of the trip, when everyone was tired and patience was thin, the children were told, "If there is one more 'Rhear" we are going home!" The chuckles heard coming from the back of the van were due to the fact that we were already going home!

After that trip, "Rhear" was added to the family vocabulary and repeated for years.

## Chapter 3

# Two Shall Become One

*Moe Becnel*

*The concept of two becoming one reminds me of the story of Abram (Abraham) in Genesis Chapters 12 through 22. God spoke to Abram, instructing him to leave his country, his people and his father's household to go to the land He would show him. At that time, Abram was living in Iraq (former ancient Babylon), which was known for worshipping false gods. When God called to Abram, the voice had to be a voice he had never heard before, since all of the idols were lifeless gods.*

*God called him out and Abram went (see Genesis 12:4), even though he did not know where he was going. His obedience required blind faith, blind trust, hearing God's voice (communication), and willingness to follow the leading of God's Holy Spirit.*

*God promised to make Abram into a great nation (see Genesis 12:2), to bless him, and to make his name great.*

*God changed Abram's name to Abraham (Genesis 17:5) and declared that he would be a father of many nations. When God told Abraham to sacrifice his son Isaac on the altar, Abram already knew that God was faithful, trustworthy, and good (see Genesis 22).*

> *God called Abraham His friend (see Isaiah 41:8). They lived life together and honored each other. Abraham had developed oneness in life with God, as did God with Abraham.* —Moe

■ ■ ■

IF YOU WERE PREVIOUSLY MARRIED, either the death of a spouse or divorce has broken the family that you and your children once had. In either case, all family members have suffered deep hurts.

But there is very good news for you and your new family. One of God's promises to His children is that He will restore us from any calamity.

> *I will repay you for the years the locusts have eaten . . .* (Joel 2:25).

After experiencing the brokenness from death of a spouse or divorce, people seek restoration of what has been lost—self-esteem, companionship, stability, financial strength, a family environment for their children, and wholeness for their future family.

God's restoration in your life and in your new family will always take place in accordance with principles found in the Bible. Before we go any further into the subject of Blended Families, we need to look at what God intended a marriage covenant to be.

## God's Principles for Marriage

Why are we discussing marriage relationships in a book on Blended Families? Blended Families face very different and very difficult challenges. Because blending a family is so difficult, 2005 statistics indicated that fifty percent of marriages and over sixty percent of remarriages with children will fail. There were many times during our first four years of marriage that Paige and I did not think we would make it.

Herein is a vital key we learned through the process, which made the difference between failure and success:

> *The strength of our new family was based on the foundation of our marriage, and the strength of the foundation of our marriage was dependent upon the foundation of our relationship with God.*

When Paige and I were not working as "one," our relationship was weak and our family was even weaker. When there was no unity between us, that lack of unity transferred into the other family relationships. When we would get on the same side, working together and supporting each other, our relationship and family began to grow. And whenever we sought God together, humbled ourselves, and followed His lead, our relationship grew strong.

I remember many days when we were not getting along, and out of desperation we swallowed our pride and went to the altar in our church for prayer. We held hands and prayed together. The only unity we may have had at the time was our physical hands joined together, but through our prayers the Holy Spirit was able to begin breaking through to our hearts—one step at a time, one day at a time, one issue at a time.

Marriage must be based on God's principles for marriage, in which the husband and wife become one. Whether your present marriage is your first, second, or third does not matter. God's principles are the same.

Let's take a look at the account of God's creation of the first family, found in the Book of Genesis.

*Then the Lord God made a woman from the rib He had taken out of the man, and He brought her to the man. The man said, "This is now bone of my bones and flesh of my flesh; she shall be called woman, for she was taken out of man." For this reason a man will leave his father and mother and be united to his wife, and they will become one flesh* (Genesis 2:22–24).

This scripture outlines three key instructions for every successful marriage—leaving father and mother, uniting to your wife, and two becoming one. While the Scripture states that the man should leave his father and mother and be united to his wife, we will discuss reasons why this principle applies to both spouses.

## Leaving Father and Mother

God has a reason for telling couples that are getting married to leave their father and mother. The above scripture identifies the potential source of a negative influence in a marriage as being parents and extended family.

God is telling us that our new marriage relationship must be stronger than the relationship with our extended family and friends. The relationship with our spouse must be more important than, and must supersede, all other relationships in our lives, except our relationship with God.

Paige and I personally know of marriages that have failed due to parental interference. We have seen marriages in which one of the spouses has never emotionally left his or her father and mother. In effect, these spouses have a divided heart with one hand in their marriage and one hand in their extended family. There is a lack of covenant relationship between the husband and wife.

Two people cannot become one if other people, such as extended family members, friends or former spouses, are allowed by one or both spouses to be involved in the decisions in their marriage.

Both spouses' relationship with their parents and others must change. The Bible tells us that extended parents and family are to be loved, honored and respected. Furthermore, parental advice can be of great value when asked for, but the married couple is no longer obligated to the extended parents.

Advice from extended family and friends is only advice when it is asked for. Otherwise, the extended family is interfering in the marriage relationship. Extended parents should never interfere in or criticize their married children's decisions. All final decisions should be made by the marriage partners.

If there is not a change in the type of relationship between each spouse and his or her parents, the marriage relationship will never become what God intended it to be.

The subject of extended families is discussed further in Chapter 7.

## United to His Wife

God instructs a man entering into a marriage covenant to unite to his wife. Webster's definition of the word *unite* is "to couple; to cause to adhere; to attach; to incorporate in one; to concur; to ally; to join in interest, affection or the like." If you were to attach yourself to a large, three-foot wide tree, it would require the use of both of your hands and arms. You could not attach yourself to the tree with one hand on the tree and your other hand holding onto something else. There would be no connection.

God has made a covenant relationship with us through His Son, Jesus Christ. God gave us His very best; He held nothing back from us in order to demonstrate the great depth of His love toward us. It is amazing that when we accept Jesus as our Savior and Lord of our life, we have a loving, living God who is attached to us and clings to us.

Likewise, spouses must make a two-handed covenant with each other. Your spouse must take the highest place of honor, respect, and admiration in your life, excepting only to your relationship with God.

> *Submit to one another out of reverence for Christ. Wives, submit to your husbands as to the Lord. For the husband is the head of the wife as Christ is the head of the church, his body, of which he is the Savior. Now as the church submits to Christ, so also wives should submit to their husbands in everything.*
>
> *Husbands, love your wives, just as Christ loved the church and gave himself up for her to make her holy, cleansing her by the washing with water through the word, and to present her to himself as a radiant church, without stain or wrinkle or any other blemish, but holy and blameless (Ephesians 5:21–27).*

This scripture describes the covenant relationship between Christ and us (the Church). Note that Jesus' relationship with the Church is to love, serve, and cleanse it. When Jesus walked the earth, He healed, taught, and loved people. He served men and women in so many ways. In this same scripture, that God-man covenant mirrors the covenant we are to hold between husband and wife. Just as Jesus gave His all for us because of His love and compassion for us, we are to develop the same "give it all" relationship with our spouse.

## Two Shall Become One

Genesis 2:24, which speaks of a man leaving his parents to cleave to his wife, is read during many weddings for good reason. I think about the vows people share with their spouses during those ceremonies. You probably remember yours vividly. But did those vows make the two of you "one" that day? Not likely. If you were already one right now, there would be no disagreements, no arguments, and no differing of opinions. I know Paige and I have not worked out every issue to our liking, and I suspect since you are reading this book that you and your spouse have work to do as well.

Rather, the vows you made on your wedding day are your commitment and promise to your spouse and to God to work to become one, and to remain faithful, true, and passionate toward each other.

The husband and wife are to become one in body, in mind, and in spirit. We all understand the simplicity of becoming one in body, but many marriages and families struggle because they never become one in mind and/or in spirit. In fact, the most unhappy marriages I have seen are those in which the husband and wife are not one in mind or spirit. They have different interests, different goals, different beliefs, different ideas, and different agendas. They do not agree on anything of significance. They do not enjoy doing the same things or, for that matter, enjoy being with each other. Nor do they support each other's dreams in life.

Please realize that spouses *must* become one. This has to be the first priority in any new marriage. Becoming one means being in one mind (harmony) and purpose (direction), and setting common goals.

Oneness may seem far-fetched or impossible, but let's look at Genesis 2:24 again. Paraphrasing, it says that if spouses will leave other people out of their relationship, and unite with each other, *then* the two will become one. In other words, doing the first two (leaving others out and uniting) brings forth oneness.

Becoming one is not the result of an event or of words that have been spoken. It is a process much like that of a small seed planted in the soil, which, with time and nourishment, becomes a mature tree.

> "Loving is not (two people) looking at each other—it's looking the same direction." —Antoine de Saint-Exupery;
> French Novelist 1900–1944

## You Are a Team

While watching any football game you will see that the quarterback on each team has one or two favorite "go to" players to whom he will pass or give the ball to more than any of the other players. I call such pairs "Winning Combinations." Those key pairs of players will put more points on the scoreboard throughout the season than any other players on the team. Examples of such pairs are:

- Joe Montana and Jerry Rice (San Francisco 49ers)
- Troy Aikman and Michael Irvin (Dallas Cowboys)
- Peyton Manning and Marvin Harrison (Indianapolis Colts)
- Terry Bradshaw and Lynn Swann (Pittsburgh Steelers)

Winning combinations do not just happen; they are not *just* two gifted players who find each other. They are pairs who do *all* of the following:

1. They have the same goals, same vision, and agree on a common strategy to make each play a success.
2. They develop relationships into friendships and spend time to-

gether on and off the field.

3. They know and work with each other's strengths, weaknesses, timing, movements, strides, and speed.
4. They study the team plays until they know them by heart.
5. They practice these plays repeatedly for months until they can execute them without error.
6. They review and study the many opponents' films of previous games in order to know each opponent's strategy, plays, star players, special teams, and where their strengths and weaknesses are.
7. They "huddle" to communicate between each play so they know what each man will do next.
8. They know they cannot do it alone. The other players on the team have to provide diversions and blocking of the opponent to create time and opportunities to complete each play successfully.
9. They participate in the team's prayer and devotional time. Many NFL teams hold devotional and prayer time before each game, asking God for protection, direction, and success.

I am convinced that God put every married couple together to be a "Winning Combination." But successful marriages do not just happen. They become successful when spouses work together as a team, applying the same commitment and effort that these football players do. Success in marriage also requires that couples lean on the support that is available to them—God's Word, God's Holy Spirit, marriage classes, parenting resources, counseling, if needed, and prayer.

It is so important for families to develop success. After all, the football players are only playing for points and salaries. For husbands and wives the stakes are much higher; they are dealing with real life and real lives. It is their responsibility to guide, encourage, and protect each other and the children, and to protect the family by stopping the adversary's attacks before damage from life crises is done.

Unfortunately, many married couples seem to be oblivious to the reality and tenacity of their adversary, the devil, who desires to defeat their family at every opportunity. They wait until a crisis strikes (the adversary has sacked them) before they decide to develop offensive and defensive strategies to combat, repair, rebuild, and protect their family.

By following the example of the "Winning Combinations" in sports, your marriage and family can become highly successful if you and your spouse are willing to apply the following principles:

- Do not do it alone. Do not ignore God. He should be in the center of your hearts and family. He has given you His Holy Spirit as your counselor and guide. Find a church that challenges you to grow your relationship with Christ, and provides support for strong marriages and programs that teach godly character in your children. Find books to edify your marriage relationship and parenting skills. Develop a deeper prayer life, praying for protection, wisdom, direction, and success.
- If you and your spouse have not already done so, purpose to develop the same goals and same vision for your marriage and family, and come to agreement on a common strategy to achieve your goals.
- Huddle—communicate daily, discussing family goals and matters. Avoid presumptions and conjectures. People often presume as a form of getting an answer or outcome. We want answers, but we are not brave enough to go to the person and ask them

for the truth about what they are thinking, why they did not return your call, how they are feeling, why they did something that hurt you, etc.

Some people are non-confrontational and will avoid communications on an intimate level. When we lack the courage to seek the truth, we presume and conjecture wrongly. Then we start thinking that we know what the other person is thinking. This leads to wrong decisions and relationship breakdown.

Talk openly, honestly, kindly, gently, and with the intent to grow relationships. Yes, communication has potential to produce tense moments and hurt feelings, but communicating to build a healthy relationship—keeping the other person's interest (not your agenda) in the forefront—will produce positive results.

If you are having trouble opening the communication channels, start with reading and studying a devotional together. It is a great step to building close communication and learning how your spouse thinks.

- Know each other's strengths and weaknesses. Paige and I are very different people, yet we compliment each other. She is strong where I am weak, and vice versa. We have come to learn that it is in the areas where we are both strong where we have friction, and we have to graciously yield to each other. You and your spouse are likely the same way. Focus on, and take advantage of, each other's strengths. Ignore each other's weaknesses.
- Spend quality time together as a couple and as a family. A couple or family devotional is a great tool. Also consider regular family meetings in which everyone participates.

- Know your adversary, the devil, and his possible strategies against you or your children. He will look for the weaknesses in your life and family. Look at the areas in which he has attacked you in the past, and determine now how you can best handle the situation when it arises again. Keep your eyes and ears open to his attacks. Do not mistakenly assume that you have no opponent facing you.

## The Bride of Christ

When I was studying the ingredients for successful relationships, God spoke these words to me:

> *"The strongest love relationship is based on mutual love, mutual honor, mutual respect, mutual admiration, mutual need, and mutual want."*

This statement describes strong acts of caring between two people. This type of relationship requires complete giving of one's self to another.

> *Husbands, love your wives, just as Christ loved the church and gave himself up for her* (Ephesians 5:25).

To understand this scripture, let's look at how Christ loves the Church (you and me), which the Bible describes as Christ's Bride. Take a moment to ponder these questions and answers:

1. Does God love you?
   Yes—so very much!

> *For God so loved the world that He gave His one and only Son, that whoever believes in Him shall not perish but have eternal life* (John 3:16).

God demonstrated His love relationship toward you by giving His best gift, His Son, Jesus Christ, as a sacrificial lamb to be atonement for your sins. God your Father saw your need, and searched heaven for the perfect gift to meet that need.

You as a Christian are part of the Bride of Christ. Jesus died so you could live, and have more abundant life.

2. Does God honor you?
   Yes! God honored you by adopting you as His child. He is the ultimate example of a loving Father in that He is your provider, protector, healer, restorer, counselor, guide, and lover of your soul. You are joint heirs with Jesus Christ of the Kingdom of God (see Galatians 3:26).
3. Does God respect you?
   Yes! God respects you so much that He put His *only* plan for building His eternal Kingdom in your hands. God does not have a contingency plan if His Church does not accomplish His plan for His kingdom (see Matthew 28:18).
4. Does God admire you?
   Yes! God must admire you, for He created you in His image and His likeness (see Genesis 1:27). Also, you are the only part of His creation to which He gave a soul that will live for an eternity. And God gave you a free will.

   He also predestined you to be conformed into the image of His Son (see Romans 8:29), and created a customized plan for your life (see Jeremiah 29:11).
5. Does God need you?
   Yes! God does not need your talents and abilities, but God needs you as a receptacle for His love. Love is not love until it is given away.

Loving you brings God fullness. He created you for His pleasure.

6. Does God want you?

   Yes! God wants you as His child and His partner. God created man to have fellowship and relationship with Him. He placed an empty place within your soul that only He can fill, so that you would seek Him and love Him. Look at how Jesus, the Son of God, came to serve man; how He latched onto twelve men to teach, fellowship with, love, and serve. In the end, He called them His friends (see John 15:15).

So God, through His Word, declares His love, honor, respect, admiration, need, and want for you. In the same way, you are to express mutual love, honor, respect, admiration, need, and want for Father God, Jesus, and His Holy Spirit.

Now, in Ephesians 5:22–25, God instructs us to apply the same relationship He has toward us, His Church, to our marriage relationship. *A husband and wife are to have mutual love, mutual honor, mutual respect, mutual admiration, mutual need, and mutual want toward each other.* A husband and wife should look for ways to bless and serve each other.

God has given you a spouse who is a jewel in your crown. Bless your spouse at your own expense.

## A Wife's Position in the Marriage and Home

God's order of creation in the Garden of Eden (Perfect Paradise) was that God made man first, and gave him responsibilities. Then God created a helper for the man.

> *It is not good for the man to be alone. I will make a helper suitable for him* (Genesis 2:18).

Man did not realize he needed help; it was not man's idea to create woman. So God made Eve from the rib of Adam to be his suitable helper. Though Eve was made from Adam's body, she was—and women still are—God's creation, made in God's image and likeness.

> *So God created man in his own image, in the image of God he created him; male and female he created them* (Genesis 1:27).

## So what is the Role of Man's Helper?

Man has defined *helper* in the workplace as "a starting position, a 'go-for' job (go get this, go do that), a grunt job, a low wage job, a low skill job, and a job in which an individual does most things a supervisor does not want to do." *Helper* implies low wages and low esteem.

In many marriages today the presumed role of the wife is similar in definition—to earn a second income in order to buy bigger homes and more stuff; to cook, clean the house, birth and take care of the children; to run errands and perform other subordinate tasks.

In fact, women are oppressed in most societies throughout the world, and are thought of and treated as inferior. The cause can be traced back to the curse God gave Adam and Eve after they both disobeyed God and ate of the forbidden fruit.

> *To the woman he [God] said, "I will greatly increase your pains in childbearing; with pain you will give birth to children. Your desire will be for your husband, and he will rule over you"* (Genesis 3:16).

Even though Jesus Christ came and broke the curses and redeemed us back to Father God, there are some men who still disrespect women or take advantage of them. For example, on several occasions over the years Paige has taken our car to mechanic shops where she was lied to, made to feel ignorant, or in other ways taken advantage of. Most women have experienced such attitudes.

## Helper Defined in the Bible

In Genesis 2:18 and 20, the word *helper* (or help-meet) is the Hebrew word *ezer*, which means "protect, surround, and aid." This same Hebrew word was used when Moses said of God,

> *My father's God was my helper; He saved me from the sword of Pharaoh* (Exodus 18:4).

In this verse, "helper" does not mean inferior. God is our Creator and is far superior to man, yet He chooses to help us. When God created woman as man's helper, He did not provide an inadequate gift. When we undervalue or mistreat anyone or anything of value, we tarnish, abuse, devalue, damage, and render that thing or person worthless—at least to us. A wife may suppress her gifts and talents because her ideas, suggestions, or other talents have not been appreciated.

I compare the successful husband-wife relationship to the relationship between me and my pastor. He and I are equal in God's eyes, but God has placed us in different positions. God made my pastor my spiritual head, so I serve the church and community under my pastor's leadership and direction. We are a "team," and we can accomplish much more together and as a local church body than if we all worked individually. So I submit to my pastor as the spiritual leader of the church I belong to. I maintain my individual relationship with God, while I retain the unique personality and talents God gave me.

I want to take a moment to speak directly to the men who are reading this book. Husbands, change your thinking about your wife. From this day forward, when you look into her eyes see the gift from God she is. See the strengths she has in the area of your weaknesses. Maybe she is the sweetness that balances your toughness. Maybe she has organization skills that you lack. Perhaps she is smarter or thinks quicker than you. Do not let those things intimidate you. Be blessed that God gave you someone who has some gifts, talents, and abilities that you lack.

See the real God-given value your wife brings to your life and family. Stop seeing her weaknesses and begin to see her real potential. If a husband is the head of the home, the wife is a crown to him. She completes him and strengthens him in the areas of his weaknesses, and vice versa. Together they become a strong team.

God placed an order in His creation, including in marriage and family, yet more than half of first-time marriages and more than sixty percent of remarriages fail today. Following are some of the reasons for this failure:

1. We decide to change God's order.
    - Some men do not take responsibility—ever.
    - Some women attempt to be the head of the home, challenging man's authority, and men concede because it is the easy road.
    - Some men do not rise up and become the spiritual head in their home. As a result, men do not protect their home from the enemy. Adam failed as he watched Eve eat the forbidden fruit, and ate some himself.

- Some women do not follow the spiritual leadership of their husband; they do their own thing. This undermines spiritual unity in the marriage.

2. We ignore the importance of God and His truth in our personal life and in our relationships. Some people believe they have a good relationship with God, but allow compromise in their marriage and family.
3. Some treat marriage as a self-serving relationship, one in which they take what they can get from their spouse and give little back.

## Husbands Love/Wives Submit

As we have met with couples over the years, the issue of submission has often come up. We hear comments such as "I don't feel loved," or "She does not submit to me."

It seems no one likes the word *submit*. Most of us, whether man or woman, like being independent and in charge of our own lives. Even the work environment can become strained when a supervisor rules over or micro-manages people. Some prefer to work together, to be part of a team, and be of equal status. Some prefer to go it alone, though that is neither healthy nor productive.

However, in marriage relationships most wives will submit to the authority of a loving, mature husband when her husband shows her respect, values her opinions, includes her in the decision process, edifies her, is proud to be with her, appreciates her as a gift from God, and enjoys her company. The partnership concept works so much better than the superior/subordinate arrangement.

Conversely, wives will have a hard time willfully submitting to someone who is harsh, disrespectful, controlling, and in other ways does not appreciate them or their worth.

Notice that Ephesians 5:22 (wives submit to your husband) and Ephesians 5:25 (husbands love your wives) were put together in the same thought process in this scripture. These two elements in marriage work together. A loving husband will draw submission, and submission gives the respect that a husband needs.

## Your Best Friend

You need to make your spouse your *best* friend. The only person I want to live the rest of my life with is my best friend.

Here is a quick test to determine if you consider your spouse your best friend. Answer the following (to yourself): When you have something good or bad happen during the day, to whom do you go or call first?

- your spouse
- your child
- your former spouse
- your mom or dad
- a friend
- a co-worker or your boss

A man or woman who does not enjoy fellowship with or find fulfillment from a loving God and a loving spouse would not have enjoyed life in the Garden of Eden (a/k/a Paradise) where Adam and Eve lived.

If your spouse is not your best friend, you need to develop that relationship. As you enlarge your appreciation for your spouse, their gifts and their dreams, you will become their best friend. A best friend helps and serves their friend. People always gravitate to the place they receive unconditional love.

Keep in mind that there is no love relationship at all when we are in a relationship merely to meet our own needs or desires. We have no love relationship with Walmart, or the gas station, or our local grocery. In the same way, we really are not in relationship with God if we only come to Him when we want or need something.

People who enter into a marriage for the purpose of having a better place to live, improving finances, filling the void of loneliness, having someone to cook and clean for them, or meeting their other needs usually wind up with a strained relationship. Acceptance and love become performance-based, and the needy (co-dependent) spouse becomes a burden to his or her mate.

Married people tend to look to each other for fulfillment, but other people were never designed to meet all of our needs. When we place expectations on another person to act a certain way or to do certain things, we only set ourselves up for major disappointment, and we damage the relationship.

Even though we are married, God must continue to be our source, our provider, and our strength. When God is our source, then we will set people free, and serve our spouses rather than expecting to be served by them.

As God meets our needs and desires, we then have a fulfilled life with which we can love and serve our spouses and others.

## Edify Your Spouse

Love is a verb—it requires action. When you love someone, the love moves you to action. Demonstrate your love; do not just tell them you love them. Show them through your serving.

There are people in my life who tell me they love me, but I do not feel that connection because there is no action that demonstrates the love. So the word *love* becomes meaningless in those instances.

If you think you are "sacrificing" to serve your spouse, your level of love for him or her is shallow. Serving someone you truly love is not a sacrifice but a pleasure.

Jesus said the second most important commandment was to love others as we love ourselves. There are two primary reasons we fail to love others, including our spouses. First, we do not love ourselves. We live with guilt, disappointments, regrets or remorse and we feel unworthy of God's love or of a blessed life. Second, we love ourselves more than others, allowing our wants and needs to overshadow those of others.

If you are not loving your spouse as you should, first ask God to help you see how He loves you. When you become aware of His image of you, His love will overtake you, and His love will begin to flow through you to others.

As you work to build your relationship with your spouse into a "best friend" relationship, consider the following thoughts:

- God made you and your spouse unique. God loves diversity. He deliberately created every person with different personalities, looks, skin color, hair, voices, accents, heights, likes, and dislikes. It is God's intent that we all be different. Do not try to change your spouse's personality.
- Never compare your new spouse with your former spouse.
- Never compare your new spouse to your father or mother. Do not expect your spouse to parent, clean, cook, or act like your parents did.
- Make every effort to not offend your spouse (your best friend).
- Add excitement to your relationship. Do different things to-

gether that you both enjoy. Try your spouse's hobbies. Avoid the "routineness" that can develop in relationships.

## Fulfilling Dreams

Paige has blessed my life in that she always knows what my dreams are, and I hear her praying to God for the fulfillment of my dreams. When our children grew up and left home, she encouraged me to get the boat I had wanted for seven years. She also encouraged me to get a new truck to pull the boat. The truck has served our household well in the years since we purchased it.

In the same way, I knew that Paige's dream was to design and custom build a home. I had built two homes before Paige entered my life, so I was not really interested in building another house or moving again. But, we purchased a piece of property a few years after we were married, paid it off, drew our own floor plan, and built her dream home in 2006.

Keep in mind that both of those tasks above took sacrifice. Paige could have desired to spend the boat money on some other family need or want. I could have said "No" to ever building another house, and come up with ten or more valid reasons.

How sweet it is when you know that you are living your life with your best friend because you help fulfill each other's dreams—serving each other.

## In the Heat of Battle

The battle of wills is never won because, in a battle of wills, someone always loses and the relationship becomes damaged. These battles are always about "self," and as they continue they cause regret and animosity. The next battle arises with the last loser feeling, "It is my turn to win."

We often hurt the very one we vowed to become one with. Every relationship has times when there are disagreements. Due to our selfishness and pride, these disagreements can escalate into damaging words and actions.

Criticism, sarcasm, and insensitivity can wound the hearts of our loved ones. Sarcasm is defined from the root word *sarcasmo*, which means "to tear flesh, like a wolf devours its prey."

Damaged relationships are not quickly or easily restored. Think back, for instance, to when you were six to twelve years old and in grammar school. (I know—it's hard for me to remember what I had for lunch yesterday!) Can you recall your mom or dad, a sibling, a teacher, or classmate who said something that hurt you? Most people can remember deep hurts and harsh words that occurred fifteen, twenty-five, even forty years ago (if you are that old).

The point is that even though much time has past, and we may have forgiven that person, those hurtful words stay with us.

Likewise, the hurtful words and actions we pass to others will stay with them.

It is this fact that makes damaged relationships difficult (but not impossible) to mend.

Guard your relationships. Protect your loved ones, especially during your own moments of anger or disappointment.

## Spiritual Battles

Almost all of our struggles in marriage and family are of a spiritual source.

> *For we do not wrestle against flesh and blood [each other], but against principalities, against powers, against the rulers of the darkness of this age, against spiritual hosts of wickedness in the heavenly places* (Ephesians 6:12).

This Scripture means that your adversary is not your spouse, a troubled child, or your former spouse. Your adversary, the devil, will use people and every opportunity to wedge his way in to damage and divide your relationships. Yet, when we become emotional we usually attack the one who is attacking us rather than attacking our adversary. When we do this we are attempting to fight the spiritual battle in the flesh rather than in the spirit.

*When we fight a spiritual battle in the flesh, we will always lose.* We may win the battle, but we lose a bit of the relationship with that person.

We must first learn how to fight our battles in the spirit, and then we must discipline ourselves to do so. When we fight our adversary, we are fighting right!

Here are some suggested ways to effectively resolve conflicts:

1. Be slow to speak; calm down.

> *My dear brothers, take note of this: Everyone should be quick to listen, slow to speak and slow to become angry, for man's anger does not bring about the righteous life that God desires* (James 1:19–20).

My translation of this scripture is, "Shut up, until you have time to calm down."

Do not say anything when you are emotionally upset. And do not push the other person to discuss an issue if they are upset about it. Allow them to calm down as well.

When emotions are high, everything is exaggerated. To a person who is highly emotional, a glass of spilled milk can become a major issue. No progress will be made when emotions are high.

2. Communicate, compromise, and work it out. Albert Einstein once said, "You cannot solve problems with the same level of thinking that created them."

   Compromising means giving, giving in, and giving up some things. Compromise is not easy; it is a skill that may need to be developed. Three steps that promote compromise are:

   - Discuss each side of the issue to gain understanding of how each person is feeling.
   - Be creative and develop some alternate solutions, other than what each of you wants. It does not necessarily have to be resolved in "your" way, or "their" way.
   - Determine which alternative is suitable to both of you, without feeling bitter about what has been given up.

   As you discuss an issue, choose your words carefully and pay attention to your tone of voice. Do not talk down to the other person, making them feel inferior, or in other ways put them on the defensive.

3. Remember, you are a team. Both of you should have the same goals. If you have different goals, make it a top priority to develop common goals, rules and discipline for your marriage and family. Doing this will prevent many future disagreements.
4. Pick your battles. Some issues are just not worth an argument. Paige and I found ourselves struggling with a few issues that were just not important, and definitely not worth an argument. We re-

alized that these instances were nothing more than pride issues; we both wanted it "my way." Let go of your pride, and let go of your "pet peeves." God did not give you those pet peeves anyway.

Again, protect your marriage. People with successful relationships are wealthy people. Winning an issue or an argument is never worth a damaged relationship. Above all, value the relationships in your life. Value the people that God has brought into your life, for they all have great value.

Jesus never tears His bride down. He is always gentle, kind, compassionate, loving, and forgiving.

> *But the fruit of the Spirit is love, joy, peace, patience, kindness, goodness, faithfulness, gentleness and self-control. Against such things there is no law* (Galatians 5:22–23).

Develop the fruit of the Spirit in your heart toward the people in your life. As you make permanent change, you will see your relationships with your family members grow.

## Strained Relationships

You may be hurting and discouraged today because your marriage is not where it should be, or not what you hope for. In Paige's and my early years we had so many unresolved issues that it wore our relationship out and created disrespect and resentment in our hearts toward each other. It was God's power that turned it all around. Our part was to stay focused on our covenant, to not quit, to keep seeking His will and His ways, and to do acts of love toward each other in spite of the garbage we were dealing with.

I learned the following things over the years:

- Bad actions and decisions damage relationships. (Bad seeds produce weeds.) Wrong reactions to bad actions and decisions make matters worse. (The weeds get thicker.)
- Hurting people hurt other people, especially those who have hurt them. Your spouse may be hurting, and may be very sensitive right now. He or she may be keeping a wall up to protect their heart from being hurt again.
- Damaged relationships are not quickly or easily restored. Relationships are not like cars; relationships do not get broken overnight and they will not be fixed in one or two days. Your hurting spouse needs time to let emotions die down, heal, and see a new you (or vice versa). It may take several months to regain trust and build security in your relationship.
- Paige and I told each other we were sorry and asked for forgiveness many times, but our relationship did not improve until each of us decided to make changes within our hearts to stop the hurtful behavior. There were traits in me that hurt Paige and her children, and I had to become determined to identify and get rid of those hurtful things. Paige had to do the same.

I love the following quotation, which I regularly use when counseling on Blended Families, because there is so much truth in it:

*"Don't judge each day by the harvest you reap, but by the seeds you plant."* —Robert Louis Stevenson

Just as a farmer plants seed, adds fertilizer, and waits patiently for—sun, rain, growth and finally the fruit, so you have to be faithful each day to plant your good seeds and wait patiently for the fruit.

Stand for your spouse and reach out to him or her. Do not lash back at him or her from your pain. Continue to display great love, compassion, kindness, gentleness, and self-control. Stay on your face before God. Ask God what seeds to plant each day—seeds for your spouse, and seeds for your soul. Keep yourself healthy and strong. At the end of each day, lay your head on your pillow knowing you planted good seed that day. God, in His time, can do amazing work with your good seed.

If the relationship between you and your spouse is damaged, here are a few suggestions:

1. Warren, a valued friend, shared a story of his marriage that had severely deteriorated. A lot of disagreements and harsh words had transpired over the years, and their relationship was very fragile. In prayer, the Holy Spirit told Warren, "Serve your wife until she turns and follows you."

   In obedience, he served, and served, and served with little or no results. After a long period of time of consistently loving her through serving her, she turned and followed his lead.

   That is exactly what Jesus does with us. He serves us even when we do not want Him. And one day we wake up and realize what a loving God we have been missing, so we then turn and accept Him as our Savior and Lord and follow Him.

2. In the movie *Fireproof*, the book *The Love Dare* was introduced as a marriage-mending tool. It is a forty-day journey of serving your spouse in order to turn your heart and to win back their heart. You can find this incredible book at www.thelovedarebook.com, or possibly at your local Christian bookstore.

3. Schedule and attend a weekend marriage conference together. There are several great marriage-building programs available. Take the initiative to rebuild your relationship.

## Our Prayer for You

God, we do not always understand the mystery of how only You can make two of us into "one" in a marriage relationship. Help the husband and wife reading this book to make each other a top priority to love each other, understand each other, and serve each other. If change needs to take place, let each spouse volunteer to let the change take place in them first. Thank You for loving this family and being in the midst of their world. We pray in the precious name of Jesus. Amen.

## Funny Family Moment

We have a few practical jokers in the family. In November of 2002, the family was at our house for Thanksgiving. Our son-in-law Charles put a rubber band on the kitchen sink sprayer hoping to spray Mom the next time she turned on the faucet. But it was our daughter Melanie who got the unexpected spray. Melanie's comment, "Okay, it wasn't funny at the time, me being a sleep deprived mom of a one, two and three-year-old, but I got it trying to fill up my baby's bottle!" What a hoot.

Chapter 4

# Divisions Within Families

*Moe Becnel*

*On one of our first dinners out as a family, Paige and I realized we had each raised our children quite differently. We went to a restaurant that provided the sealed "one-tablespoon" liquid coffee creamers set out on the table. My two children each grabbed one, opened it, and drank it. Paige objected and said those creamers were for people who bought coffee. I rebutted, saying I allowed my children to have one or two. We had several arguments over those two tablespoons of coffee creamer, as well as over other different views we had about raising children. We were off to a great start as an un-united family!* —Moe

▪ ▪ ▪

MANY BLENDED FAMILIES do not function as a united family, rather they exist with multiple divisions or fragments within. Spouses who are not working together, children who do not want to be in or do not feel they are a part of the family, hurts from extended family, and disagreement over rules and discipline are a few of the many issues attacking these families. Words and phrases like "his children," "her children," "my rules," "your rules," and "you discipline yours and I'll discipline mine" are common to Blended Families.

Our adversary, who is as real as we are, has all types of families worldwide on the defense. Many families have been pushed back to the goal line with Satan ready to score a victory over them. Today, too many marriages and families are struggling. They live with hurts, offenses and/or bitterness as they deal with seemingly uncontrollable or rebellious children, and they see no way out.

Too often, parents stick their heads in the sand and assume all is well, or hope that the situation will somehow fix itself. Such thinking ensures failure because it opens the door for the enemy to defeat Blended Families.

> *The thief comes only to steal and kill and destroy; I have come that they may have life, and have it to the full* (John 10:10).

> *Be self-controlled and alert. Your enemy the devil prowls around like a roaring lion looking for someone to devour* (1Peter 5:8).

The devil's plan has always been, and continues to be, to kill, steal, or destroy anything that is of great value to God and God's prized creation, mankind. He seeks to harm . . .

- our relationship with God (mostly through distractions, compromise, or other false religions),
- our marriage,
- our family,
- our children,
- our grandchildren and
- our life.

He has already destroyed some of our first marriages, and has left many of us with deep hurts, children who are broken, and many more extended family members who are wounded.

The devil has some special tools that he uses exclusively on Blended Families. As a result, Blended Families face significantly more challenges than biological families. God warns us of Satan's age-old plans in the Bible.

> *. . . in order that Satan might not outwit us. For we are not unaware of his schemes* (2 Corinthians 2:11).

Satan had the Becnel family on the defense until, through prayer, God began exposing the devil's playbook. You see, our adversary is not very creative. He has been using the same old plans to kill, steal, and destroy for thousands of years. The only new twist comes when he focuses his plans on you and your family.

In this chapter, we will show you some of the strategy our adversary used to come against our family. We will also show you how God helped us fight back and gave us the victory.

Be aware that there are three plans for your life. God has a plan. You may have a plan that is different from God's. Your adversary has his plan. Just as Father God uses people to build His kingdom, provide blessings to us, and speak into our lives, our adversary also uses people to try to accomplish his plans in our life. I know he has in the past used my temper, anger, and opinions to damage many of the important relationships in my life. I also know that my plans that were not in agreement with God's way have often not turned out good.

My ultimate goal is to get myself (and my baggage) out of the way, stop the enemy's destructive work, and see God's perfect plan established in my life and family. I hope this is your goal, too.

## God's Principles for Families

We must emphasize to husbands and wives the need to be on the offensive—fighting for your family. The Becnels learned the hard way that nothing took care of itself if we just ignored it and hoped for the best. We had to get on the offense by seeking and applying God's principles, and working to develop the character of Jesus in each family member. Likewise, your strategy has to be intentional and deliberate.

Let's begin by looking at some of God's principles for families. God created the first family when He created Adam and Eve in the Garden of Eden. According to the Bible, God was present with Adam and Eve in the Garden. God was in the midst of their life.

It is God's plan to be in the midst of your life—to make your new family a true family, built on strong relationships and filled with unconditional love. Only the love of God can make this happen. God wants to be in the midst of the re-creation of your family, and God's hand must be in it.

> *Unless the Lord builds the house, its builders labor in vain* (Psalm 127:1).

We cannot successfully build a loving family and home without God's help. His principles are necessary to achieve His design for a family.

If you have received Christ as your Savior and Lord, you already have a head start. God's Holy Spirit already lives inside of you. It is up to you to utilize that incredible, supernatural resource for the building of your new family. It is your will—your choice—whether you choose to engage God in your marriage and family. We pray that you make the right choice on a daily basis, asking for God's guidance in every decision (see "God's Love and Plan for You" in Appendix A).

## Divisions Within Families

Matthew 12:25 describes a problem facing every struggling family today.

> *Jesus knew their thoughts and said to them, "every kingdom divided against itself will be ruined, and every city or household divided against itself will not stand"* (Matthew 12:25).

These are powerful words from Jesus. Satan's main strategy is to look for a place to divide the marriage relationship. When he finds that weak spot in the relationship and begins his work, the erosion of the marriage and family begins.

Erosion is a slow but deadly process. Years and years of daily rain, storms, raging rivers, glaciers dragging across mountains, and freezing weather cause the crumbling of solid structures. Erosion has created drastic crevasses such as the Grand Canyon, reshaped entire mountain ranges, and deteriorated the pyramids. It is a fact that newer mountains have jagged peaks, while the older mountains have rounded tops due to erosion.

In the same way, repeated exposure to negative words and behavior, insults, harshness, criticisms, verbal abuse, passive or aggressive rejection, and so on will severely damage hearts and erode your family, and even your life or the lives around you. Consider the following questions:

- When do occasional drinks progress into alcoholism?
- When does trying an illegal drug grow into an addiction?
- When does the first glimpse of pornography become a compul-

sive lifestyle?

- When does repeated anger escalate into uncontrolled verbal or physical abuse?
- When does a hobby become a compulsion?
- When does the enjoyment of good food become obesity?
- When does an office friendship turn into an affair?
- When do frequent arguments between a husband and wife escalate into disrespect and resentment?
- When does discipline by a stepparent become resentment in a child's heart?
- When does hurt in a teen's life escalate to isolation, depression, or suicide?

All of the above are examples of what can happen through the erosion process—erosion of our thought process, our emotions, and eventually our will. People lose control of their own will. Their emotions take control over their sound judgment, and their life is led by ungodly thoughts and uncontrolled emotions. Life gradually yet surely turns into what seems to be a death spiral, taking its victim further away from making right choices (righteousness)—and seeing no way out.

Many divorces have occurred through the erosion process. The marriage relationship deteriorates to what seems, at least to one spouse, to be a point of no return.

If a husband and wife allow divisions to remain between them or within their home, the erosion process will begin and the marriage and family will eventually fail. At times all families, biological or blended, allow divisions to become established. Because divisions are usually established subtly, we may be unaware of some of the divisions in our home. But the hairline cracks created by differing opinions, conflicting family goals, lack of teamwork, arguments, insults, offenses, disrespect, and pride, among other things, can erode into bigger and bigger divisions.

Realize this: All divisions are the work of our adversary, the devil, for the purpose of destroying the family, or destroying our life.

Typical areas of division in Blended Families include:

his children vs. her children
his beliefs vs. her beliefs
his ways vs. her ways
his opinions vs. her opinions
his rules vs. her rules
his discipline vs. her discipline
his extended family vs. her extended family
his money vs. her money
his wants vs. her wants
his goals vs. her goals
his pride vs. her pride

Divisions may already exist in your family, even if you do not think they do. If your spouse sees divisions, they are either really there or at least perceptually there. If your children see them, they are there (or perceptually there). And they will remain until you and/or your spouse make changes.

Remember, perception is reality. If your spouse perceives a division, it must be addressed—either by proving their perception to be incorrect, or by resolving the issue.

Ask for examples of what they perceive. Ask for evidence. Practice empathy; put your feet in your spouse's shoes and try to understand it from their point of view. Discuss it thoroughly.

## Symptoms of Issues

The following are some symptoms of issues in Blended Families. Take note to see if there is any "unblendedness" in your home.

- "You discipline yours and I'll discipline mine" are common statements.
- You only speak with pride of your biological children.
- You only talk about your children, while your spouse only talks about his or her children.
- Your spouse's parents and/or siblings do not accept you.
- You have high grace toward your children, but low grace toward your spouse's children.
- Two sets of rules exist in the home (his children vs. her children).
- Two sets of expectations exist in the home (his children vs. her children).
- You and your spouse have not decided on one set of rules and discipline.
- Children call the new parent by "Mr. or Mrs. (name)."
- Your one-on-one time with children is spent only with your biological children.
- The term "step" is used within and outside of the home (stepfather, stepmother, stepson, stepsister, etc.).
- You feel as though you are raising someone else's children.
- Your grown children are not a vital part of your new marriage.

- One or more children may have opposed your remarriage.
- Your spouse has grown children, whom you do not consider a part of your life.
- "They have other parents" is your excuse for not treating your spouse's children with acceptance.
- You do not love your spouse's children as your own, nor do you think you can.
- You think, "My spouse's children do not want me in their lives."
- You do not consider your spouse's grandchildren as your grandchildren.
- Child support is not used to support the intended children.
- You and your spouse have separate checkbooks.
- You and your spouse disagree about the use of child support.
- There are "favorite" children in the home.
- A former spouse is allowed to interfere with your new marriage and family.
- You or your spouse do not feel secure in your marriage relationship, or with your home environment.
- You have feelings of dislike, anger, or resentment toward one of your spouse's children.

Keep in mind that these are only symptoms of the real issues, just as a cough is a symptom of something wrong within our respiratory system. Even if many of these symptoms exist in your home, do not lose heart. Many of them existed in our home, as well. The good news is that you have identified some areas that need work in your family.

Throughout the rest of this book we will peel the onion to show what the causes of these symptoms are. Then you can take action, get on the offensive, and start making your house the home that God intended it to be.

You must resolve divisions. Until they are settled, the divisions will continue to breed arguments, which creates a domino effect that looks like this:

- Repetitive arguments will breed harsh words.
- Repetitive harsh words will create offenses.
- Repetitive offenses will develop disrespect.
- Ongoing disrespect breeds resentment.
- Long-term resentment manifests hatred.

We will now look at some of the divisions that existed in the Becnel family, and tell you how God directed us to handle certain situations.

## Establish Order and Respect for the New Parent

It is natural for parents to want to protect their children, especially if the children have been hurt through the death of a parent or by divorce. There is a strong tendency for biological parents to nurture and protect their children in a new family, even to the point of going against the new spouse.

Children in a new Blended Family may not be emotionally ready for, or like, the new family environment or the new parent. A child may see the new parent as an outsider who is not only taking their parent's time away from them, but is now disciplining them as well. Children may attempt to manipulate, challenge, and bring division between their parent and his or her new spouse in order to get what they want.

Manipulation by children occurs in all homes to some extent, but in the Blended Family environment the child often challenges or attacks the new parent's authority. Children may make statements such as:

- "You love him more than me."
- "I wish we were a single parent home again."
- "You always take your new wife's side."
- "You are not my dad."
- "I am not your responsibility."

Children may also attempt to maintain the natural parent relationship to the extent of excluding the new parent from any responsibility for, or involvement in, their life.

The reactive response by many biological parents is to side with their child, protecting the child's feelings and desires, and eventually placing the child in the place that rightfully belongs to the new spouse.

## God's Order Within the Family

We realize that children are very important to the biological parent. We are advocates for children of divorce. We understand (though perhaps not fully) what divorce and remarriage has done in the lives of our five children, and we strive to teach parents to help their children to heal. However, God has an order for every marriage and family. That order is:

- God is the center and foundation of the home.
- The husband is number one—the head of the home.
- The wife is number two—partner, helper and best friend.
- The children are number three.

And that order does not change regardless of whether the home is a first, second or third marriage. When we attempt to change God's order through our own reasoning, we mess up and cause the marriage and home to suffer.

Ask these questions to your spouse:

1. "Do you feel I show my children more respect than I show you? If yes, give me examples."
2. "During the times I have shown my children more respect than I have given you, how does that affect your attitude . . .
   - regarding our covenant marriage?"
   - regarding your place in our new home?"
   - toward the stepchildren?"
   - toward me, your spouse?"

   If you are giving your children the second place, I think you will find that your spouse will object to, and eventually resent, those children who have been given, or who are attempting to take, his or her rightful place in the covenant marriage. And that objection or resentment will also transfer to you for letting the child have that place.
3. "Do you believe our children are running our lives and marriage?"

   If a child is given second place, then the child is given a co-leader position by the biological parent, and is, in essence, running the home. The child is coming between the husband and wife. There can be no clinging or cleaving to a new spouse if a child is standing between the two.

*Therefore, what God has joined together, let man not separate* (Mark 10: 9).

Many children have been allowed to separate a husband and wife (parent and stepparent), creating yet another divorce. Another divorce is not what your children need to experience. They need to experience proper order and a loving home so they can reproduce a loving marriage when they grow up and marry.

Here is a great testimony. We met a family who was struggling with this order issue. The husband was not allowed by his stepchildren to have any part of their life, and the children were very rude and disrespectful toward him. The couple decided to apply the "proper order" and established it in their home.

The wife sat down with each biological child and explained the following: "God is number one in my life. My husband is number two. And you are number three. Number three is not a bad place. I will continue to love you as my very own, provide for you, embrace you, vacation with you, live life together with you, and in every way take care of you. The only time being number three becomes a problem for you is when you challenge for the number two position by disrespecting my husband. I cannot make you love him, but I demand that you treat him with respect."

In that conversation with her children, she was explaining to each child the order that God (not the new parent) mandated in the home and that the family order was about position, not about love.

After that conversation, the family began to unify. The children *finally* knew their position and boundaries. They actually began to respect their new parent and, over the next few years, grew to love him.

Many children have challenged the proper order issue as a love issue with comments such as, "You love them more than you love me." Using the same example I stated earlier, God loves my senior pastor and me equally. The Bible says that God is no respecter of persons, but God has given us different positions in the same church in which we serve together. Since God appointed him as senior pastor, I submit myself to him and follow his lead.

The number two and number three positions in the home are very similar. It is not a love issue at all, though your children may perceive it that way, or may try to manipulate you into thinking it is. We are establishing proper order in the marriage and family. Once the children know their place and are taught to abide there through encouragement, instruction and reward, the family will be successful.

For further reading on the proper order within the family, read the book, *Kid CEO—How to keep your children from running your life* by Ed Young; Pastor, Fellowship Church; Dallas, Texas.

## Your Marriage Covenant

Love your spouse to the same extent you love your biological children. As we previously discussed, in Ephesians 5 the Bible tells husbands to love their wives as Christ loves the church, and there are nine verses that fully describe that command. Then there are five verses of instruction to the wife for her relationship with her husband.

The marriage covenant is so important to God that it was the first thing He mandated after He presented Eve to Adam. Do not look at your remarriage as a second marriage. Look at your remarriage as an outpouring of God's grace on your life; your second chance to have a first-class marriage. You have to strive to develop that great marriage covenant.

## Respect Is Two-Way

The establishment of proper order in the home is probably the hardest area of all to overcome, and requires a great deal of courage on the part of both parents. Spouses must stand up for each other in front of the children, even when they think their spouse is wrong.

The biological parent must demand that his or her children be respectful of the new parent figure, thereby establishing the proper order in the home. You cannot make your child love another person, but you can require that they treat your new spouse with respect. There should be a rule set regarding proper respect, and appropriate discipline should be outlined for when the rule is broken. Your child should know the rule and the discipline, so that they know what is expected of them and the result if they do not comply.

When you disagree with how your spouse has treated or disciplined your biological child, a discussion with your spouse about the matter needs to be conducted alone, away from the hearing ears of the children, away from home if necessary.

Teaching your children to have respect for your wife or husband, their new parent figure, is a must, and it starts with your example. If you show signs of disrespect for your spouse, your children will never grow to respect him or her.

We must not forget that respect is earned; it is a two-way street. If we want others to respect us, we need to give respect. New parents (stepparents) need to give respect to their new children.

Crystal, a reader on our website has a great signature line. She signs her name as follows:

*Crystal*
Mother of 4
Two by Birth
Two More by God's Grace & Wisdom

This statement displays great respect for the new children in her life, and her loving commitment to them.

We show respect to our children and stepchildren when we . . .

- spend time with them doing what they like to do,
- listen to their concerns, thoughts and ideas,
- help them develop their talents and abilities, and
- engage ourselves in their lives.

## Action Steps

- Stand up for your new spouse and demand that your biological children respect him or her. Failure to do this will cause your new spouse to resent both the new children and you.
- Establish proper order in your family, explaining it to your children as an order of position, not who Mom or Dad loves more.
- Discuss areas of disagreement between you and your spouse away, far away, from the children.
- Do not spoil children because they are children who experienced divorce or death of a parent. I agree that your children are hurting from the previous broken home, and possibly from rejection by the other biological parent. But lack of discipline and letting them get away with misbehavior only makes matters worse.
- Stepparents should look for creative ways to show respect to their new children. Listen to their ideas, take them on outings,

spontaneously buy them small gifts (an ice cream cone, gum), and praise them for doing something you asked.
- Until they have had time to adjust, handle children with great kindness and grace.

## Validation Process

Almost daily in life we meet someone who is trying to validate themselves. If someone does not really understand their identity in God, their insecurities cause them to attempt to establish their identity through displays of authority, assertiveness and name-dropping. People validate themselves when they assert their wealth, position, title, level of education, material possessions (the biggest house), their heritage, social circles, or power over others. In all these things they are attempting to draw attention to themselves.

Individuals in your new family may be attempting to validate themselves in some fashion. In the process they display the content of their heart: love and acceptance, past or present hurts and frustrations, fear, insecurity, or anxiety.

Teens display validation more clearly than any other age. Bill and Amy had a Blended Family with a teen daughter who for weeks came home from school, went to her room and locked her door. She did not come out to eat or socialize with the family. She was likely validating that, although she may have to live in that house, she refused to be a part of the new family environment.

Other examples of validation behavior are as follows:

- A new parent may begin the discipline process with new children to establish rules, position and authority in the home.
- A child may cling to the biological parent and compete for his or

her attention in order to validate that the relationship has not been weakened by the new marriage.

- A child may compete with other siblings to establish position and roles in the new home.
- A child may excel in school to win favor with Mom, or grades may drop to seek the attention they are not receiving.
- A new parent may try to be the mom or dad to the new child, but is rejected by the child. The child is validating that they are not yet ready for that relationship.

So the atmosphere can become trying, even tense, when dealing with hurting, insecure people. Jesus knows all about that. Remember, He came to heal the broken hearted.

A family member's validation behavior may be interfering with the growth of your new family, but you can be the positive influence that breaks through the hurt.

The way to overcome the adverse validation process is to stop trying to validate who you are, and help each person in the family validate who they are in Jesus Christ. In Christ each person is . . .

- forgiven for their wrongs through the grace of God, when there is repentance,
- accepted as a son or daughter by God,
- an heir with Jesus to the Kingdom of God forever,
- loved unconditionally, just as they are,
- given purpose for their life that will last for eternity and
- given gifts, talents, and abilities.

When we begin to understand who we are to God and how much He loves us, we are on the path to being healed of our hurts and insecurities. Once healed, we lose the need to validate who we are to others. We then develop a desire to love others as God loves them and extend His grace to them. Competition disappears and compassion develops. This is why having Christ in the center of your home is so important to the health of every family member.

## Action Steps

- Identify any negative validation you are exhibiting, and stop it. Assist your children in doing the same thing, letting them know that they are loved for who they are.
- Get your family plugged into a dynamic Christian church that will help each family member to grow and mature his or her relationship with God.

## "Step" Syndrome

The primary objective of a Blended Family is to establish a loving, caring relationship between everyone involved. Our words have the ability to bring life or death to our relationships. There are words that can undermine how close a relationship will develop. We have found that the widely used terms "stepmother" and "stepfather" automatically puts, and keeps, the new parent in a separate, and usually lower, category than the biological parent. The same applies to the terms "stepsister" and "stepbrother."

Several years ago our son came home from church and was upset. When we asked what was wrong, he said one of his new sisters had introduced him to some of her friends as "my stepbrother."

A few years ago we purchased a new refrigerator and had it delivered to our home. When the deliveryman and his helper got out of his truck, he innocently said, "Hi I am Ted, and this is my stepson Eric." As soon as I glanced at Eric, he hung his head. With just one word, he disconnected.

When Jesus came to earth, He brought the New Covenant to God's chosen people, the Jewish nation. After Jesus' resurrection, God commissioned the Apostle Paul to preach the Gospel to the Gentile nations. Thus, the Gentiles also became God's children. The Gentile Christians did not become God's stepchildren while the Christian Jews remained God's children. If God called me His stepson, I am not sure what I would expect of Father God compared to what His biological sons would be entitled to. I am so blessed that the Bible declares that I also am God's child and joint heir with Jesus Christ to the Kingdom of God.

The word "step" can bring confusion, build walls, and develop different levels of belonging, acceptance, and ownership in relationships. Use of this term places and keeps the new relationships within the home in a separate category. Each time the prefix "step" is used, it declares, "I live with you, but we really do not belong together," or "You are not my 'real' child." It segments the family.

## Words of Belonging

We all have a need to belong and to find unconditional love. So shouldn't we avoid using words that keep distance between us and others?

The Becnel family decided to not use the term "step" either within or outside our home. We introduce all of our children as "all of our children" because, in our hearts, they are.

Some couples introduce their new children as "my bonus children," "my bonus daughter," "my new son," or "my children by God's grace." That expresses much more kindness and acceptance.

When Paige and I were married, we gave our children the option of calling us Moe, Paige, Mom, Dad, or a nickname. Our younger children wanted to call us Mom and Dad, and have done so since. Our oldest daughter called Paige by her name, and did so for the first eleven years of our marriage. That was fine since that was comfortable for her. During our twelfth year together, she started calling Paige "Mom" and has done so since.

As loving relationships with new children grow, the new children may want to call the new parent Mom or Dad or other terms of affection. More than simple names, what you are called by children can express affection, acceptance, and belonging.

We encourage parents to not let the children call their new parent names such as Mr. Pete or Mrs. Amy. Mr. and Mrs. are formal terms that are not conducive to family relationships. Some people have argued that Mr. or Mrs. shows respect to elders. I agree, and I was raised to address my parent's friends as such. But I did not address my grandparents, aunts, or uncles in that way because they were family. Family is family and should be treated as such—so drop the formality and build your family.

## Belonging in the Other Home

What if a child's other biological parent objects to his or her child calling someone else Mom or Dad? What if you are hurt by the idea of your biological child calling another adult Mom or Dad?

I can address these questions from personal experience. When my children began calling their mom's new husband Dad, I was hurt and very upset. I felt my rights as a parent were being stolen. But eventually I realized my attitude was due to a hurt that needed to be healed so I could let the issue go, if for no other reason than for the happiness and well-being of my children. My children needed to experience a loving home atmosphere with their mother, as well as in my new family.

Remember, you should not attempt to control what goes on in someone else's home any more than you should allow someone else to control what goes on in your home. Consider your child's use of an affectionate term for his or her new parent in their other home as a blessing—a sign that your child is finding comfort and stability in life.

Rest assured that even if your biological child chooses to call the new parent in the other home Mom or Dad, you will always be the biological parent—a bond that cannot be broken. With the exception of yourself, no one places more importance on the parent/child relationship than your child. You will always be their biological parent, and they know it.

## Objections from the Other Side

Within your home, take the pressure off of your children. If the other biological parent strongly objects to your child wanting to call their new parent Mom or Dad, let the child choose a nickname. Nicknames are also terms of affection and closeness. Our grandchildren call Paige and me Toots and Papa. These are nicknames for the traditional Grandma and Grandpa. A nickname will work well in the bonding of your new family. Forcing the issue of having the new children call you Mom or Dad only puts unnecessary pressure on the child.

## Action Steps

- Stop using the prefix "step" when referring to, speaking to, or introducing family members to others.
- Help the children to develop and use names of affection in your home.
- Do not object when children have names of affection in their other home.

## You Discipline Yours, I'll Discipline Mine

We know of many Blended Families in which the husband and wife continue to function as single parents.

In most new blended homes, an initial effort is made to blend the role of parenting between the biological and new parents. However, the blending of these roles can be very frustrating, and frequently the parents will decide to retreat from that effort in order to reduce friction in the home. Many families have found it easier for each biological parent to take care of their own children. So the resulting theory, "You take care of and discipline your children, and I'll take care of and discipline mine," is common in Blended Families.

Is this theory acceptable? No, because it effectively sets up the home as two single parent families living in the same house, and ultimately undermines the order and authority that God established in a family.

The easy road of coping is usually not the right road. It is an issue in the family and if it is not removed it will build disrespect and resentment between the new parent and the child, as well as between the husband and wife.

We experienced the frustration and felt the rejection and disrespect between new parent and new children caused by the inappropriate "you discipline yours" process. It truly divided our home and our marriage relationship. Here are six reasons why the "you discipline yours" family undermines itself:

1. The role of the husband and wife in a home is to become one and work together to support the children in that family, including disciplining them. When this role is retracted from the new parent, he or she will likely begin to feel disconnected from that family because the role they are to fill has been removed. The disconnect will eventually deteriorate the marriage and family relationship.
2. The new children will likely sense a victory over the new parent, and the new parent/new child relationship will never develop as long a competitive spirit exists between them.
3. When the new parent is not allowed to discipline, the children are being taught that there is something wrong with their new parent, and that they do not have to listen to, or respect their new parent. Thus, it hinders building strong relationships between the new parent and new child. We will discuss "earning the right to discipline" in the next section.
4. Having two separate authorities and rules (his child/her child) in a home is damaging to the home. It sets the stage for favoritism. When two sets of rules and two discipline methods exist (one child is allowed to do something that another is not, or one child is punished more harshly than the other), it will likely cause the children to compete with each other or resent each other.
5. "You discipline yours" causes disunity in the home. God's order in the home is for husband and wife to work together as a team. When husband and wife are not operating in one mind and purpose, it will cause all family members to not want to connect to

that family or to each other.

6. It hinders the home from developing into a loving environment. A peaceful loving family develops out of a flow of unconditional love among all family members. When there is a lack of love by any member of the new family, it creates stress in the home rather than peace.

If you and your spouse are not working together to function as a family, the children will not try either. They are looking to you for guidance. You and your spouse must bond together first. The children will respect your efforts and follow suit.

## Earning the Right to Discipline

A husband and wife may enter into a Blended Family as new parents and assume that they now have parental authority over all the children in the family. Not so—at least not right away.

Discipline administered by a new parent who does not yet have a loving relationship with the new children is most often harsh, and usually causes hurt feelings. Repeated harshness will lead to disrespect and resentment. *Love must supersede discipline.*

> *Because the Lord disciplines those he loves, and he punishes everyone he accepts as a son* (Hebrews 12: 6).

This scripture tells us that God disciplines and punishes those whom He first loves and accepts as sons and daughters. What does this mean for us as new parents? Unless, or until, we truly love our new children and accept them as our own sons or daughters, we have no right to discipline them.

"Wait a minute," you might say. "If they are going to live under my roof, I have a right to discipline them."

I understand how you feel and I believed that way also, but hear me out. When you were a child or a teenager, if someone other than your parents tried to discipline you, what did you do, and how did you react? You probably thought something like, "What gives him the right to tell me what to do?" or "You are not my parent!" You may have already heard these words in your new family.

Yet, you accepted discipline from your mom or dad. Why? Because they loved you, and you knew they loved you.

Your new children will react the same way you did to discipline coming from someone other than your parent. We must, and will, *earn* the right to discipline our new children as they experience our love for them.

When we get it backwards, meaning when discipline supersedes love, the implication is, "When you do what I say, then I will love you and show you respect." This is called "conditional love," which is not really love at all, but is actually tolerance. Discipline without love is no different than discipline in the Army, or from a police officer, or from a teacher or coach. When discipline or punishment is dispensed without love, it is often stern and rough. The result is that respect fades and resentment builds. We repeat . . . love must supersede discipline.

When we discipline with love, we automatically operate with mercy and grace, not harshness. There is *gentleness* to our expectation. When true love is applied, moments of grace will surface where we occasionally let children off the hook because our love for them flows.

Many new parents believe their spouses do not discipline the biological children hard enough. This belief is caused by the following four possible reasons:

1. The parent is a poor disciplinarian.
2. The parent does not discipline because of feelings of guilt.
3. The parent is extending God's compassion and grace toward the child.
4. The new parent has little or no compassion because the new parent/new child love relationship has not been established.

Of these four, the fourth is the prominent reason. In my thirty years of being in relationship with God, He has disciplined me many times, but He has never done so in a harsh manner. The Holy Spirit has never offended me, called me ugly names, or in any way put me down. God's Spirit is always gentle, always kind, and always forgiving. God always has my best interest in mind. On many occasions Father God has spared me from getting what I truly deserved, and I know He has done the exact same thing for you. After all, if we got what we deserved, Jesus would not have gone to Calvary to redeem us from our sins.

As you develop the loving relationships with your new children, showing the children that you accept them and want them in your life, you will earn the authority, the position of leadership in the home, and the right to discipline them. Then you will have the ability to discipline with gentleness and grace—even willingly sparing them from what they deserve at times.

## The New Parent's First Year, or Until . . .

There is a transition time when new parents need to not discipline, or retreat from enforcing discipline, and spend time and effort to build valued relationships with all the children.

During the first year of marriage (or until the new parent has built successful loving relationships with each new child) when the new child misbehaves, new parents should express the reason and the need for discipline to their spouse, and let the biological parent administer any needed instruction and discipline. Biological parents should allow their spouse to participate in the parenting process, but at least during the first year the biological parent should carry out the discipline. The first year is the time to be the fun new parent.

## Build Healthy Relationships

All families are built one relationship at a time. In biological families, this process happens through the birth of, and bonding with, children. As we attempt to build a Blended Family, the principle is the same, but the strategy is different. As new parents, we need to be intentional in building relationships with our new, already-birthed children. In the same way we spent hours and days getting to know and fall in love with our new spouse, we need to develop the relationships with all the members of our new family.

This takes time, effort, and patience. There are no short cuts to building relationships—you already know the effort it takes to have a great relationship with your spouse. The same time and effort applies to the relationships you need to have with your new children.

Building relationships with new children is even tougher because the child may not be interested in a relationship with you or in the family. Yet, that barrier can be overcome as you let those children know that they are important—to you and to the new family. There are positive steps in the process. Do not be in a hurry for this to happen. It is a slow but steady process. Give relationships the time they need to grow.

The more quality time you spend with your spouse's children, the more you will start to love them, and the more love and respect they will have toward you. Remember, love is a choice. You must choose to love your entire new family. You, the new parent, have to make the time and effort; doing so is not the children's responsibility. Change starts with you, the adult.

As we stated earlier, the first year is a time to be the fun parent—to be goofy and crazy with the children, to talk with them about things they like, take them places and enjoy life with them. It is a time to become their friend and someone they can trust.

Do not fall into the pit of thinking that the children are not important and not worth your time. First of all, realize that all children are a blessing from God. Secondly, know that if you choose not to bond with your new children, you will stop the growth of your new family, the children will not feel that they are a part of the home, and strife can rise.

We have noticed that in some families, new parents who have no biological children often have a much harder time in wanting to build the new parent/new child relationships. They seem to lack patience with children and can be intolerant of immature, child-like behavior. Bonding with the children can be challenging to them. Some such parents seem to never be able, or are just not willing, to make the transition. These situations may require parenting classes, the power of prayer, and the benefits of a counselor.

## Rules, Discipline and Timing

Many couples have not developed one set of rules for their new home. These families continue to struggle with whose rules are being applied, and whose discipline gets implemented. Perhaps they are caught in the "you discipline yours" style. Perhaps they have tried to come up with one set of rules, but opinions, selfishness, and stubbornness have prevailed. In either case, two sets of rules still exist.

Many of the family struggles will stop when the couple becomes determined and intentional to sit down and develop one set of rules for their home, which will apply to all children, and appropriate discipline for each rule broken. Once the new set of rules and appropriate discipline are established and written down, a family meeting should be held to inform the children of the expectations in the home, and the resulting consequences when not followed.

Then, as we just discussed the need for love to supersede discipline during the first year of marriage (or until the new parent has built a successful loving relationship with each new child) when the new child misbehaves, the new parent should express the reason and the need for discipline to their spouse, and let the biological parent administer any needed discipline. Biological parents should allow their spouses to participate in the parenting process, but at least during the first year the biological parent should carry out the discipline.

## Action Steps

- For parenting styles, the two of you need to sit and develop one new set of rules and one discipline that is agreeable to both of you, and will apply to all children in your family. If you are unable to compromise between your two former family systems, find a parenting resource that teaches a philosophy that you both can agree with. Our recommendations are *Parenting Is Heart Work* by Scott Turansky and Joanne Miller (visit www.biblicalparenting.org) and *Growing Kids God's Way* by Growing Families International (visit www.gfi.org). Write down your agreed-upon rules and stick to them. Don't make excuses for your children when they break the rules. Be consistent with everyone.

- The new parent should be intentional and persistent to build relationships with each new child. This takes time. Develop a regular schedule for spending some fun time alone with each new child and getting to know them, their personalities, their likes and dislikes. Just showing interest in them goes a long way. One-on-one activities and attendance of school functions and extracurricular activities with each new child will build the relationship.
- Be intentional in building loving relationships with your new children. By doing so you will earn respect, authority, and the right to discipline. Be patient.
- Biological parents should allow the new parent to participate in the parenting process, but at least for the first year the biological parent should carry out the discipline.
- If you have biological children but your new child misbehaves, ask yourself, "How would I respond if this were my biological child?" This step serves as a "grace-meter." Make every effort to treat your new children as you do your own and extend grace to them.

## Favoritism

Favoritism exists within a home when parents treat individual family members differently. Favoritism is a symptom of different levels of love (i.e., a father spends more time with his son than his daughter, or a mother shows more attention to her biological children than her spouse's children), or of feelings of guilt.

The story of Joseph, the eleventh son of Jacob (Israel), as told in Genesis Chapter 37, shows the damage that favoritism does to a family. Jacob had twelve sons. The following verse identifies a major problem in their family:

> *Now Israel loved Joseph more than any of his other sons, because he had been born to him in his old age; and he made a richly ornamented robe for him. When his brothers saw that their father loved him [Joseph] more than any of them, they hated him and could not speak a kind word to him* (Genesis 37:3–4).

As the story continues, all the brothers plotted to kill Joseph, but then decided to sell him as a slave to a caravan going to Egypt. They told Jacob that Joseph had been killed by a wild animal, and gave him false evidence by applying goat's blood to their brother's garment. The following are noteworthy points of this story:

- Jacob, the parent, created the favoritism.
- Jacob's family looked very different after he gave the robe to Joseph. Favoritism turned to jealousy and eventually created hatred, deception, and loss within the family.
- The brothers took their resentment out on Joseph, not on the father who created the favoritism. The brothers still longed for the father's affection and did not want to damage that relationship.
- The brothers put goat's blood on Joseph's *richly ornamented robe*, which was the reminder of the offense, and gave it back to Jacob, their father.

Favoritism can occur in all types of families, but it is more pronounced in Blended Families where bonding of the family has not yet occurred, and may not occur for a few years. People tend to love their biological children more than a child that was not born to them. And as stated before, a parent controlled by guilt will show favoritism to their biological children.

Different rules, different levels of mercy and grace, and inconsistency in discipline in your home will generate jealousy and resentment. You must treat all the children in your home the same.

## Action Steps

- Agree that the need to treat everyone in the family equally is of great importance.
- If you have not already done so, take time, paper and a pen, and work out an agreeable set of new rules and discipline that you and your spouse can live by, and that apply to all the children.
- Agree that any required discipline will be administered equally. When grace is extended, it must be extended equally to everyone.
- Always treat everyone the way you want God to treat you with great levels of compassion, mercy, grace, and forgiveness.
- Show equality to all children in your giving of gifts and time.

## Submission After Independence

As we mentioned in Chapter 1, adults who have been living a single-again life with children due to the death of a spouse or divorce have had to become independent and self-sufficient for themselves and their children. This in itself is good. We are sure these single parents have learned, as we did, just how strong, independent and self-sufficient we can be when we have to be, and how God's provision takes care of us through those times.

However, when a single parent remarries, he or she is often confronted with an equally independent, self-sufficient spouse who has conflicting ideas, likes, dislikes, opinions, ways, and rules for the new home. It is not easy to give up our way of doing things when we have been living independently and satisfactorily for a long time. And of course, the older we are the more set in our ways we become.

All successful relationships require giving. Jesus Christ, the ultimate giver and servant, is the role model for our lives. Each spouse has to learn to be flexible and to give of themselves and their ways to their spouse and new family. They must be willing to agree to solutions that work for both spouses.

When you are married, you are no longer on your own. You have committed your life to others. Things no longer have to be done your way. Give yourself and your ways to your spouse and new family.

Yielding to each other shows respect for and allows each person to blossom in the relationship. Appreciation for each other grows, and love increases.

If you are at an impasse where neither spouse is willing to give, an unbiased third party can help mediate a solution. This mediation process can teach the couple the art of creativity, compromise, and working for the best decisions of the family.

Keep in mind that your goal is a peace-filled, loving home. Standing your ground is contrary to achieving unity. For additional help, please read "Resolving Conflicts" in Appendix C in this book.

## Action Steps

- Give, give in, and give up your ways so that one set of new, agreed-upon rules, not just your rules, can be established.
- Brainstorm possible alternate solutions to the issue at hand without discounting each other in the brainstorming exercise. All ideas are to be written down and discussed without putting each other down.

## Child Wants Biological Parents Back Together

Many children of divorce live in a domicile home with one biological parent, and they miss their other biological parent when they are not with them. Almost every child-of-divorce has a dream to see their biological parents reconcile, even after one or both are remarried. And they may hold on to that dream for many years—even into adulthood.

We know of children who have attempted to sabotage one parent's remarriage in the hopes of getting Mom and Dad back together (similar to what happened in the *Parent Trap* movie, but without success). We have seen a child break down on his mom's wedding day, even though his dad was already remarried.

And we have met adult children who, although their divorced parents had remarried many years ago, have not been able to let that dream die and thus remain disconnected from their parents' new marriages and families.

It is of utmost importance that we understand that the fulfillment of our dream to remarry and start a new life often becomes the death of our children's dream to see Mom and Dad reconcile.

This is a huge struggle for many children. Children need time and opportunity to understand, let go of old dreams, grasp new dreams, allow the relationships in the new family to develop, and accept the new family environments. Be honest with your children, repeatedly explaining the situation with patience and loving-kindness.

## Action Steps

- If your child is showing signs of a hurting heart, extend grace and be gentle. Explain that although you and your former spouse will not reconcile, the child is still very much loved. Explain that the divorce was not the child's fault.
- Assure your child that you will never leave them. Perhaps in their mind one parent has already left, so they fear you might also do so.
- Allowing a child to participate in the new home with roles and responsibilities can help bring healing, helping the child feel a part of the new family.
- Make your child aware of the benefits of the new family—every cloud has a silver lining.

In Chapter 5, we will more thoroughly address Blended Family issues from the children's perspective.

## Child Wants to Live with the Other Biological Parent

Parents may find themselves faced with a child who wants to leave the domicile home to go live with the other biological parent. There may be two basic reasons for such a desire.

Reason 1: Perhaps the child simply misses the other parent, or the other parent is persuading the child to come live with them. Should this child then live with the other parent, he or she would probably begin to miss the parent he or she was previously living with. If possible, we strongly encourage both biological parents to work through this with the child. The goal is not for one parent to win over the other, but to develop an arrangement that everyone agrees upon. However, frequently bouncing a child back and forth from one home to the other should be avoided, as this arrangement fails to develop stability in the child's life.

Reason 2: The child may want to leave the domicile home because he or she does not feel wanted or accepted, or feels that he or she is not a part of the domicile home. Perhaps the child does not get along with the new parent, or there is friction between new siblings, or the child does not like the new family's set of rules. Such situations call for tender loving care.

Realize that most people, including children, will not want to leave a place where they feel loved. In fact, people migrate to the place where they find unconditional acceptance.

Should this situation arise with your new children, be sensitive toward your spouse. Losing a domicile child will cause heartache for your spouse. Imagine how you would feel if your child wanted to leave your home.

If you are the new parent and there is tension between you and your new child, or between your biological children and your new child, you must take action. You are the adult. It is your responsibility to help the child feel loved and to know he or she is vital to the family.

Love your spouse's children. They are an integral part of your spouse's life. If you do not love your spouse's children, you do not truly love your spouse. Your spouse and children were one before you entered the picture. You cannot separate them. Failure to love the children will only cause further division in your marriage and home.

If a new child leaves to live with the other biological parent because of tension or rejection from you, your spouse will resent you. You will have caused the separation of a relationship between your spouse and his or her child, a relationship that is vital to them.

## Action Steps

- If Reason 1 exists in your home, talk with your child to uncover their true feelings. If possible, work through this issue with the other biological parent—with input from your new spouse.
- If the child does not feel a part of the new family, as in Reason 2, the real issue must be uncovered and resolved. If the new parent does not love the child, the new parent must take responsibility to develop a relationship with the child. The new parent/new child relationship is equally as important as the husband/wife relationship.
- Work to resolve any new sibling conflicts.

## Your Spouse's Need for Security

Another area that Paige and I struggled with was insecurity. Both spouses must feel secure in the marriage relationship, and certain things I did—albeit unintentionally—threatened Paige's security.

The greatest of these actions involved conversations that took place between me and my former wife concerning our children. I was certainly not trying to make Paige feel insecure, but I was not treating Paige as my covenant partner in the way I handled the situations, and tended to not stand up for my new family.

If your relationship with your former spouse is threatening to your new spouse, it is your responsibility to do whatever is necessary to make your husband or wife secure. I changed the format of my conversations with my former spouse, and made no decisions about my children until I discussed the issue with Paige. After all, every decision I made about my children would affect Paige's life—our time together, our weekend or vacation plans, our finances, their school, their extracurricular activities, their medical care, and so on. So Paige deserved to have input in the discussions about my children. Your spouse also deserves the same respect when it comes to discussions about your children. We understand that there are certain situations where court orders must be followed and we are not encouraging you to circumvent legal issues or requirements.

A second area that tested the security of our relationship involved our house. After the wedding, Paige and I resided in the house that my former wife and I had built. Paige struggled to make this house her home. At first I thought Paige would get used to the house and the feelings she had about the house would simply go away. (Ladies, men are really slow thinkers at times, or we can just be insensitive!) But this was not the servant attitude God wanted me to have toward my wife. Instead, we agreed to make some changes—new room colors, wallpaper, curtains and bedspreads that reflected Paige's personality and taste.

We have heard from other Blended Families that have had the same struggles of both men and women dealing with feelings of insecurity. Many sold their homes and purchased a home that was new for their new family, or bought new furniture (even at garage sales to stay within budget), and had other creative ideas.

Other actions that I needed to alter included my frequent fishing and hunting trips, and my failure to take up for Paige when people (including family) were rude to her.

By this point, you may be thinking that Paige was being possessive and controlling. I can assure you that this was not the case. She was merely pointing out things that made her feel uncomfortable, unvalued or unwanted. Through my actions or inactions, I had made Paige feel that other people, hobbies and things were more important to me than she was. I realized that my actions or inactions were harming the growth of our relationship, and that husbands are responsible for making their wives feel secure.

How did we address these areas? With common sense.

## Action Steps

- We understand the realities of paying alimony and/or child support. Your new spouse will, too. But beyond that, your devotion and resources must be toward your new spouse and new family. Any additional resources that you direct to your former spouse or children must be with your spouse's agreement.
- Your home should be a reflection of you, your spouse, and your new life together. Make sure both spouses' personalities and tastes are reflected in your home.
- No relationship, job, sport, hobby, or activity should be more important than your relationship with your spouse. Take inventory of your life, and determine what is hindering the growth of your marriage covenant.

As you give you will receive, and receiving always carries a multiplication principal—you will receive more than you gave. The more you invest in your marriage relationship and your new family, the greater you will receive, not only from that relationship, but from God as well.

Love, respect, dignity, honor, want, and high esteem are earned only through investment in relationships. These are the treasures that your spouse and family will give back to you when you choose to serve them.

In our case, I had to learn not only to give, but to give in, and to give up certain things. Did I quit hunting and fishing? No, I did not have to. Once I demonstrated that Paige was more important to me than these activities, she became secure. I continued hunting and fishing in moderation, sometimes accompanied by Paige and our children. Those family outings turned into great family times and memories that we still talk about today. But most importantly, I realized there are much more valuable things in life.

Do not be overwhelmed with what you have read in this chapter, or with the issues you have identified. You, your spouse, and God are more than enough to achieve greatness in your family.

## Action Steps

- Discuss the divisions you have identified in your own family with your spouse. More may surface as you proceed through this book.
- Pick the top three areas in your family that need work, and work on those. Do not try to do too much at one time, or you will become frustrated.
- Do not expect too much too soon. As we said before, families are built one relationship at a time. And relationships take time to build, especially with any family members who are hurting.
- Plan a family activity together when all are available to attend.

## Brick Walls

We faced many complex issues, which we have come to call "brick walls," in our family's first four years together. No matter how many times we dealt with an issue, it never seemed to go away. The repeated frustration made us want to quit on many occasions. We have learned a few things about brick walls.

- Brick walls can make us want to quit, but do not quit.
- Brick walls are not as resilient as we are. They cannot stop us, but they let us know how bad we want something.
- Brick walls show our passion and determination for something, or lack thereof.
- Brick walls will draw blood when we try to knock them down in our own way and in our own strength.
- Brick walls do fall when we come against them with determination, tenacity, perseverance and the supernatural ability that comes from God's wisdom and power. They cannot stand against the breath of God.

## Our Prayer for You

Father, we know that families are built one relationship at a time. We ask You to touch this new family as they take the time to nourish each other and grow together. By Your favor, allow all of the relationships in this family to grow. Help them establish love and grace as the foundation of that growth, and gentleness as the foundation of discipline.

As they work together, show this couple a strategy to address each issue. Bring light on their darkness and new life into their new world.

We thank You for giving us Your mercy every day, Your love as a foundation for us to work from, and Your favor with You and with people. We also thank You for Your wisdom, guidance, and breath that changes our lives.

In the powerful name of Jesus. Amen.

## Funny Family Moments

Jordan was a junior in high school when he asked for a guitar for Christmas. I envisioned that after three or four months the guitar would be tucked away in a closet, so Paige and I talked him into getting something else, and he did. After all, no one in our family had musical talent. After Christmas we were at Paige's sister's house, and we told them the guitar story. Our brother-in-law, an accomplished guitarist, went to his bedroom and came back with an old Yamaha acoustic guitar, which he gave Jordan. Within six months, Jordan and a friend self taught themselves thirty praise and worship songs. He began playing for the church youth band, and began to sing. Today his chosen career is that of a worship leader.

It is so amazing how God will accomplish His plan in our children's lives, in spite of our "we know what's best" parental attitudes.

Chapter 5

# Ingredients for Healthy Blended Families

*Moe Becnel*

*We started leading the singles ministry at our church in December of 1995. As recently divorced single parents came to the group, we would recommend and refer them to a divorce recovery program at another church, even though neither Paige nor I had previously attended such a class. In 2001 our pastor asked us to develop a divorce recovery program for our church. We did, and began leading the twelve-week class, teaching half of the classes ourselves and bringing in outside speakers to teach the other classes.*

*During the first program, as we taught some sessions and listened to the other speakers, both Paige and I each learned so much about ourselves. Each of us realized that we had unresolved issues in our hearts from our previous divorces, even after having moved on in our lives and being married to each other for twelve years.*

*Though we had seen a noticeable level of success in the blending of our family (evidenced by our children's eighth anniversary gift to us), through these classes the Holy Spirit was showing us that we could achieve more. We realized there were some unresolved issues, invisible toxic baggage, we had been carrying and that baggage was holding back the health and growth of the loving family we were so earnestly trying to build.*

*During the next couple of years, Paige and I began the painful process of unpacking our own personal baggage. (There are times when the content of one's heart is not a pretty sight.) As we each began the process of taking this critical step, additional sustained growth began to take place in our family.* —Moe

▪ ▪ ▪

IN CHAPTER 3 we identified and discussed some issues that can cause significant problems in a marriage and Blended Family. In this chapter we will cover certain positive aspects of relationship building, which are part of all successful marriages and Blended Families, each of which are key ingredients to building healthy, solid, loving relationships.

## Individual Wholeness

Before constructing a new home in Southeast Louisiana, where our soil is soft and water-laden, numerous thirty to forty foot long wood pilings (treated tree trunks) are driven into the sand strata beneath the ground to provide a solid foundation for the house. In areas with better soil, deep trenches are dug in the ground beneath the place where the walls will be built, and these trenches are filled with concrete when the slab is poured. These "footings" support the weight of the walls and roof structure and keep the house from sinking.

In the same way that the strength and stability of a house depends on the soundness of its foundation, the health of a new family greatly depends on the spiritual and emotional health of each spouse and family member. We call this "individual wholeness."

Our son Jordan recently shared the following story with Paige and I:

> "I remember in the beginning of our new family developing, home wasn't always a peaceful place. It would get very heated in our household between my dad and my new mom, so heated at times it was very scary for me as a young child. The tense arguments were so loud and magnified to my ears that it terrified me. I would think, 'Here we go again,' or even, 'I don't want to get yelled at.'" —Jordan

Jordan's statement made Paige and I realize how much additional pain we had added to the lives of our children in the early years of our marriage as we struggled to build a new family. Our children did not deserve the broken biological homes and two families they now had, and they certainly did not need to be in an unsettled new home.

We now look back and can see clearly that Paige and I got married too soon. What do I mean? Most of the *tenseness* in those "*tense arguments*" in our early years were harsh responses created from previous hurts and rejection that we were both feeling from our divorces and the resulting anger, frustration, and unforgiveness we had not yet been healed of. Those pent-up, suppressed negative emotions were rising up in our disagreements and spilling into our new marriage and onto our children. And what was spilling onto our children was creating much damage.

Yes, we had Blended Family issues that we were dealing with, but our unhealed hearts caused us to handle the issues in very unhealthy ways, which resulted in damaging the people and relationships within our new family.

In the mid 1980s there were no divorce recovery programs available. Pastors did not know what to tell us or how to direct us to find healing from the pain of divorce. Today there are many Christian resources available for divorce recovery, children of divorce, grief recovery, addiction recovery, anger management and many other self-help areas. (You should research the resources to determine which are the best.)

Individual wholeness is defined as being secure as an individual, knowing who you are to God and knowing who God is, or wants to be, to you—your Father, provider, protector, deliverer, and healer.

God called Himself "I AM" (see Exodus 3:14). Among other things this means God is whatever you need Him to be, every day and in every situation in your life, because He is able, and He is your most excellent Creator and Father. No person on earth, not even a husband or wife, can fill that role in your life. Individual wholeness includes our being healed from past hurts, failures, and disappointments. I would describe an individually whole person as having the following traits:

- Calm spirit
- Confident
- Content
- Disciplined
- Good habits
- Happy
- Looks for good in others
- Loving
- Peaceful
- Positive
- Productive
- Self-sufficient with God

If you are not individually whole, you have nothing to give to your spouse, to your children, or to your new children. Rather than trusting God to be your provider, you are dependent on another person, probably your spouse, for your happiness and the meeting of your needs. The result of this kind of dependence is, you become a taker in the relationship, and you wind up being disappointed.

Children also need to be individually whole in order to live a peace-filled, content life. And until they find their own healing and wholeness, it is likely that the children will subconsciously create strife in their world. We will further discuss the children in Chapter 5.

## Fellowship with God

God created us not only with a body and a mind, but with a spirit that allows us to fellowship with Him. The spirit part of man is vital, and man goes to great lengths to fill that part of life. Consider the many different religions of the world, all seeking to fill and serve the spirit man.

When the spirit is empty, the man or woman is empty. People who do not know God and who reject religion will try to fill that emptiness with work, hobbies, habits, busyness, and physical relationships. When we try to fill our spiritual emptiness through relationships with men and women, we always come up empty and disappointed.

Wholeness in each of us (including our children) comes only when the spiritual part of our lives is fulfilled, and only Jesus Christ can restore us to Father God and fill that void in our life.

> *I am the way and the truth and the life. No one comes to the Father except through Me* (John 14:6).

## Intimacy Is Fellowship

Intimacy is a word that gets most people's attention. If there were a blank space in front of that word, most people would fill in the blank with the word "sexual." But intimacy is far more than sexual. There can be intimacy in friendships.

The best definition of intimacy I have heard is this: "to truly know someone, and to truly be known." Don't we all want to be intimate—to truly know someone, and to truly be known? This is true of all people, regardless of age, gender, financial status, or geographical location.

People usually only reach a closeness in their relationships that is dictated by past experience. If, as children, they did not experience relational intimacy with their parents, their future relationships will have unspoken, preset boundaries.

Similarly, many people have a distorted view of Father God's love for them because they may have only experienced conditional love in the home they grew up in. They subconsciously reason in their mind and heart, "No one can love me more than my parents did."

We have heard people say, "God does not care about me," or "God is punishing me," or "God is not interested in me." But when we search for Father God through His Son, Jesus Christ, we find Him and we experience His true love and forgiveness. Through relationship with Christ, people experience what true unconditional love really is, perhaps for the first time in their life.

God made a great effort to be intimate with you when He showed up through His Son, Jesus, who is teaching, loving, caring, preaching, and healing you and your family in order that you may:

- *behold* Him,
- *partake* of Him,
- *experience* His endless, unconditional love,
- *understand* His compassion, mercy, and grace toward you and everyone around you,
- *really know* what God meant when He said, "I will be their God, and they will be My People" (see Jeremiah 32:38; Revelation 21:3).
- *gain* His infinite wisdom and counsel,
- *listen and do* what He tells you for your good,
- *be healed* in body, mind, and spirit and live in wholeness,
- *trust* Him with all your concerns and decisions.
- *find and fulfill* His purpose for you, and
- *behold His power* to change your world.

God is always faithful to do His part in our relationship with Him, but, we also have a part to play. Following are three important points about intimacy with God:

1. Intimacy with God is all for *you*. He is all for you. He loves you so deeply. When you become intimate with God, you experience His unconditional love, daily mercy, and abundant grace in your life. So why is time with God usually the first thing to be pushed off the plate when we get busy? Seek to know Him in a deeper way than you have ever known Him.
2. If you are too busy for God, you are too busy. It is time to prioritize your life and get rid of unnecessary things.

> *And you will seek Me and find Me, when you search for Me with all your heart* (Jeremiah 29:13).

As with any relationship, building your fellowship with Jesus requires time and devotion.

3. Your intimacy with God will infiltrate your marriage and family. His wisdom will become your wisdom. His compassion will influence your compassion for others. His character will become your character, and will positively impact your spouse, children, new children, former spouses, extended family, and every other relationship in your life.

   As you continually develop His heart within you, you will more freely pass that type of patient, kind, and servant-minded love to your family.

## Be Set Free

You may have experienced past hurts through broken relationships (from death, divorce, or break-ups), personal failures, business struggles, severe illness, or other sources. Or you may be struggling with one or more habitual moral issues that are damaging to relationships with God and man such as pornography, adultery, gambling, excessive drinking and such. God needs time to heal your hurts and your heart, preferably before you move into another marital relationship. If you are remarried and still carry hurt, anger, bitterness, low self-esteem, resentment toward others, past trauma, other negative attitudes from your past, or any damaging relationship behaviors, those negative feelings will affect everyone around you today and into your future.

Now is the time to be set free. Jesus has a gracious way of delivering and restoring us when we have experienced pain, hurt, failure, or we feel we have failed God. Remember these truths about God:

- He does not condemn us.
- He does not criticize us.
- He does not humiliate us.
- He does not harm us.
- He does not even think bad thoughts about us.
- He continues to love us, even when we are not lovely.
- He renews His mercy and grace to us each morning.
- He guides us to a righteous life.
- He gently seeks our heart and asks us to reaffirm our love for Him.

God looks at each individual and sees potential, not failure. God also promises to heal our hurting hearts. Isaiah 61:1–3 speaks of the coming Messiah, Jesus Christ:

*The Spirit of the Sovereign Lord is on me,*
*because the Lord has anointed me to preach good news to the poor.*
*He has sent me to bind up the brokenhearted,*
*to proclaim freedom for the captives*
*and release from darkness for the prisoners,*
*to proclaim the year of the Lord's favor*
*and the day of vengeance of our God,*
*to comfort all who mourn, and provide for those who grieve in Zion—*
*to bestow on them a crown of beauty instead of ashes,*
*the oil of gladness instead of mourning,*
*and a garment of praise instead of a spirit of despair.*

*They will be called oaks of righteousness,*
*a planting of the Lord for the display of his splendor.*

Today, begin to build your intimate relationship with your Heavenly Father through a relationship with Jesus Christ. Look to God as your source of healing and individual wholeness, and set yourself, as well as your spouse and family members, free.

To learn more about how you can have intimate fellowship with God, see "God's Love and Plan for You" in Appendix A.

## A Widowed Heart

After fourteen years of marriage, Mary's husband, Walter, died in a boating accident. She and her children lived in a single parent family for three years and grieved the loss of their husband and father. Mary met Steven and after a time they were married.

One year after their marriage, Steven confided in his best friend, saying, "Mary must still be in love with Walter because she constantly talks about what he did for her, the places they vacationed together, the furniture he built, the things he did with their children, and so on." Steven went on to say that not only did Mary keep pictures of Walter in the house, but when they were with friends, he often overheard Mary talking to others about Walter.

Steven felt very disconnected from, and unloved by, Mary.

A widow or widower who remarries may find that they struggle to let go of the love they have for their deceased spouse. In such instances, the widowed person likely has not yet fully grieved the loss, and may sense confusion between the two marriages since they still feel a part of both of them. When this happens, the result is that the new marriage is strained. In the example above, Mary's actions displayed that her heart was still devoted to Walter (although she may not have realized what she was doing).

In other situations the widow or widower may sense guilt over feelings of love for their deceased spouse, so the widowed person keeps his or her feelings within. Yet, keeping feelings inside only exasperates the situation and their new relationship. The new spouse likely senses the divided heart of their spouse caused by this polarity.

A person who is still grieving loss may want the companionship and other benefits that the new marriage offers, but they have nothing to give to the new marriage or new children. Entering a new marriage may become a way to temporarily fill the void the widowed person feels, but it drains the new spouse. Ultimately, the widow or widower must grieve the loss and be healed in order for the new marriage to survive and thrive.

Consider this thought: If you are a widowed spouse, you and your deceased spouse may have been deeply in love, and he or she might have been a great parent and role model. For some reason, your loved one's life was cut short (from illness, an accident, fighting for our country, violence, or other) and they finished their life's race early. Yet, God, in His wonderful grace, has brought you another spouse to continue the same race your former spouse was running with you. In effect, your new spouse has taken the "baton" from your former spouse in loving and caring for you, as well as in loving and caring for your children. Allow your new spouse to fulfill the race that you asked him or her to run with you on your wedding day.

The Apostle Paul speaks of striving toward what is ahead:

> *Not that I have already obtained all this, or have already been made perfect, but I press on to take hold of that for which Christ Jesus took hold of me. Brothers, I do not consider myself yet to have taken hold of it. But one thing I do: Forgetting what is behind and straining toward what is ahead, I press on toward the goal to win the prize for which God has called me heavenward in Christ Jesus* (Philippians 3:12–14).

In Apostle Paul's case, his purpose was to be a witness for Christ and build the Kingdom of God. If you were widowed and have since remarried, one of your purposes is to build the new marriage and family that you vowed to build on your wedding day.

We know how hard it is to forget the past when we are still hurting from the past. In 2 Corinthians we read that Paul had some great trials, disappointments, and persecutions in life.

> *Are they servants of Christ? (I am out of my mind to talk like this.) I am more. I have worked much harder, been in prison more frequently, been flogged more severely, and been exposed to death again and again. Five times I received from the Jews the forty lashes minus one. Three times I was beaten with rods, once I was stoned, three times I was shipwrecked, I spent a night and a day in the open sea, I have been constantly on the move. I have been in danger from rivers, in danger from bandits, in danger from my own countrymen, in danger from Gentiles; in danger in the city, in danger in the country, in danger at sea; and in danger from false brothers. I have labored and toiled and have often gone*

*without sleep; I have known hunger and thirst and have often gone without food; I have been cold and naked*
(2 Corinthians 11:23–27).

Wow! So many intense difficulties and afflictions would be enough to stop most men and women from moving forward. Paul's secret to keep building the Kingdom was his understanding that he had to keep looking forward. He knew that dwelling on his past would defeat him. So his message to you and I is the same—stop looking back because it will defeat us, and instead look toward the new goals, the new plans, and the new relationships that God has brought into our life.

Although the pain from Paul's difficulties, rejection, and life circumstances may be different than the pain one feels from the loss of their former spouse, both were legitimate pain. And the only solution to bring forth the abundant life that Jesus came to give us is to grieve our loss and look forward.

Until healed, the widowed person should do his or her best to give the highest place of honor to the new spouse. If you are a widowed person, here is what you can do:

- Consider your new spouse more important than yourself.
- Talk more about your new spouse than you do about your former spouse.
- Never compare your new spouse to your deceased spouse. Respect the individuality that God gave your new spouse.
- Allow your new spouse to express love in his or her own way.

## To the Widowed Person's New Spouse

If you find that your new spouse is still attached to, and grieving over, the deceased former spouse, do not fight or push for love, affection, and attention that he or she is emotionally unable to give at this time. Until your widowed spouse has grieved and healed, you should continue to serve your grieving spouse. Be patient, compassionate, and understanding. He or she will heal.

This same scenario applies to a child who has lost a parent to death. The child may now be in a Blended Family, but their heart is disconnected because of the grieving process. Extending a serving heart toward the grieving child by the parent, stepparent, and siblings is needed, along with patience, compassion, and understanding. Allow them to grieve. Help them find grief recovery resources. Be a part of their healing process.

## Learning from Your Past

As stated in Philippians 3:12–14 above, the Bible tells us to stop living in the past and look forward to the new things God has in store for us. However, we need to learn from our past mistakes and failures so that we do not continue to have repeated failures.

One of the classes we developed in the Healing Place Church divorce recovery program was called "Mirror-Mirror on the Wall." The objective of the class was to help people look at themselves and identify any damaging relationship behaviors or habits still existing in their lives. The purpose of this exercise was to prevent people from damaging future relationships in the same way that they may have brought damage in former relationships.

An excerpt from the "Mirror-Mirror on the Wall" class has been included in Appendix B; we are sure it will help you grow.

## Action Steps

- Assess whether you are individually whole. Do past hurts or failures still trouble you? Ask a close friend or family member to give you an honest assessment of any negative behaviors or emotions they see in you. If yes, seek help from a pastor or counselor, or get some self-help materials. Ask the Holy Spirit to show you the path, the people, and the resources He will send to help you heal.
- If you are remarried and still have feelings for your deceased spouse, grieve the loss so your new relationship can grow. Attend a grief recovery class or find and read some grief self-help books. If necessary, seek professional counseling.
- Help your grieving child to heal.
- Begin to look forward—look at the new things, opportunities, and people God is bringing into your life.
- Review "Mirror-Mirror on the Wall" in Appendix B and make notes of any relationship improvement skills you can make. Be honest with yourself.

## God as the Center of the Family

There is so much truth to the statement, "The family that prays together stays together." If God is truly made the center of the home, the home will prosper. The following scripture is a fundamental principal of living a fulfilled life:

> *Blessed is the man who does not walk in the counsel of the wicked or stand in the way of sinners or sit in the seat of mockers. But*

*his delight is in the law of the Lord, and on His law he meditates day and night. He is like a tree planted by streams of water, which yields its fruit in season and whose leaf does not wither. Whatever he does prospers* (Psalm 1:1–3).

What an awesome promise to those who walk with God. Now consider this same scripture and how it would apply to a family that lives for God. Let's take that scripture and replace the word "man" with the word "family," "that family," or "family's."

*Blessed is the [family] who does not walk in the counsel of the wicked or stand in the way of sinners or sit in the seat of mockers. But [that family's] delight is in the law of the LORD, and on His law[that family] meditates day and night. [That family] is like a tree planted by streams of water, which yields its fruit in season and whose leaf does not wither. Whatever [that family] does prospers* (Psalm 1:1–3, modified).

What is the message in the modified scripture? The family who delights in the law of the Lord prospers. As a husband and wife seek a daily, loving relationship with God, allowing God to take control of their hearts and lives and establish a Godly standard in their home, they will prosper, and as a direct result, their family will also prosper.

Successful families establish a high standard of righteousness (right choices) and excellence in their homes, with high expectations. Parents are responsible to set goals to achieve a godly standard in their home, and to identify obstacles that hinder the accomplishment of those goals.

If you are not already attending church as a family, start now. Find a church that your children enjoy, and where you and your children will be challenged to follow the principles of God. Send them to every children's camp, youth camp, and retreat.

Again, read and study the Bible as a family. Use a daily devotional and let the family discuss their thoughts on the day's message.

## An Orderly Home

The Almighty God and Creator of the universe is a God of order. All of God's creation is put together intricately and perfectly. Consider the human body. Every organ, gland, and appendage has a specific purpose, and is positioned to serve that purpose. If just one organ stops functioning, the whole body becomes sick and possibly dies.

The level of detail God gave Noah to build the ark and the instruction God gave Solomon for building the Temple even down to the type of material and color for each item—reflect God's attention to detail and order.

Disorder prevents a home from functioning as a place of love, nurturing, and security. A disorderly home lacks peace and joy. Husbands and wives have a responsibility to pursue order in the home.

In Chapter 3 we discussed God's order for the hierarchy for every marriage and family.

- God is the center and foundation of the home.
- Husband is number one—the head of the home.
- Wife is number two—partner, helper and best friend.
- Children are number three.

Yet, proper order in our marriage and family goes further than this. What is, and is not, reflective of order within a family? First of all, it is *not*:

- a family with regimentation, enforced with strictness.
- a family with no leadership, no rules, and/or with no discipline.

On the other hand, it *is*:

- a family with two loving, considerate, patient, kind parents/new parents.
- a family who loves God and lives by high moral standards.
- a family devoted to building the relationships within.
- a family with one set of rules, and with discipline when rules are broken. Rules have no purpose if they are not consistently enforced.
- a family with respectful, obedient children.
- a family with reasonable schedules.
- a family with goals, and strategies for accomplishing those goals.
- a family with a neat, clean, organized residence. External appearance often depicts what is inside a person; the same can hold true for a family.
- a family in which the order of leadership in the family is God as the foundation, husband is the leader, and wife as the husband's partner, helper and best friend.
- a family that includes God as the center of the home through church attendance, church involvement, Bible reading and study, and seeking God's guidance over marriage and family decisions.

## Train a Child

We have met several parents who allow their minor (underage eighteen) children do as they please. In some cases young children are allowed to make decisions for their life that will adversely affect their future. There is a culture in our society in which parents take more of a friendship role than a parenting role in their child's life. Many parents take on the role of entertaining their children rather than being a parent to them. Children are too immature to make sound decisions for their life; this is why God put them under the care of parents.

> *Train a child in the way he should go, and when he is old he will not turn from it* (Proverbs 22:6).

This scripture is a standard for all parents, both biological and new. The word *train* means "to instruct by practice; drill; discipline; educate." Sports teams become winning teams when, during training, they learn plays and will practice them until they can execute them without error.

In the same way, training children is more than teaching or telling them what to do. It is showing them what to do and being the example to them. Ultimately, children will do what we do, say what we say, and act as we act.

Here is some guidance of appropriate training for children:

- Teach them to pray and include them in your family prayer time. Let them hear you pray for them and others.
- Take them to church with you. Do not ask them if they want to go; they do not understand the importance of knowing God and His Word. Also, do not "drop them off" at church. Show them that God is important to you, too.

- Give them small responsibilities around your home, and show them how to do them well.
- Help children find their God given gifts, talents, and abilities and help them develop these gifts.
- Be a living example and teach your children the principles of character—honesty, determination, integrity, perseverance, patience, kindness, faithfulness, encouragement, gentleness, compassion, and love.

## Care to Not Exasperate

In Ephesians Chapter 6, the Apostle Paul gives valuable instruction to parents about raising children.

> *Fathers, do not exasperate your children; instead, bring them up in the training and instruction of the Lord* (Ephesians 6:4).

*Exasperate* means "to provoke to anger, to annoy, or to irritate." To exasperate anyone is to do the opposite of the true nature and heart of God. What is God's nature and heart?

> *But you, O Lord, are a compassionate and gracious God, slow to anger, abounding in love and faithfulness . . .* (Psalm 86:15).

We have already discussed many ways that parents and new parents in Blended Families may exasperate the children. Some would be harsh discipline, yelling, putting down their efforts, using children as a pawn, passive rejection, not valuing their thoughts and ideas, how one parent interacts with the other biological parent, and lack of time and attention. Continuous provocations can wound a child's spirit and cause them to become discouraged and timid.

Parents need to become conscious of words and actions that may provoke the children, and make needed changes to eliminate the addition to our children's pain.

## Giving

As we have stated before, relationships that last are giving relationships.

God gave. We are God's children because God gave His Son, Jesus Christ, to restore us back to relationship and fellowship with Father God. Likewise, we are to live a life of giving. Unfortunately, we have been programmed by a selfish society. Television, newspaper, and magazine advertisements are designed to increase our wants and to feed our selfish desires. Most marriage and family disagreements can be traced to selfish wants and acts. The number one cause of divorce is selfishness.

Creating a loving family requires the opposite response—a *selfless* lifestyle. Husbands and wives, your family blessings will come according to the level of your giving. Throughout the Bible, God teaches the principles of giving and receiving, and sowing and reaping.

> *Give, and it will be given you. A good measure, pressed down, shaken together and running over, will be poured into your lap. For with the measure you use, it will be measured to you* (Luke 6:38).

Notice that the giving precedes the getting. As we give, we receive. It never works the opposite way. As you give into the lives of your new family, you will receive blessings from God. The receiving process usually does not happen quickly. But do not stop giving. God's Word is faithful and true.

One day when Paige and I were struggling over an issue, neither of us wanted to give up our position, or give in to the other's wants. I felt I had already given enough, and that it was Paige's turn to give. Then God spoke these words to my thoughts:

> "Until you are on your knees and have washed her feet, you have more to give, and you will only receive in accordance with your level of giving."

Ouch! God had exposed my flesh, pride, and selfishness. Jesus did not hesitate to wash His disciples' feet. He *wanted* to wash their feet; it was an act of loving. The water in the basin was insignificant—Jesus was washing His disciples with His incredible love. *Jesus was declaring that there was nothing He would not do for them.*

Love requires action, and that action is giving. This includes giving in, acknowledging that things do not always have to be done your way. Here are a few simple ways you can give of yourself to your new family:

- Determine your spouse's desires, ambitions, and dreams. If possible, help your spouse accomplish them.
- Find out about your children's likes, dislikes, and hobbies. Learn their friends' and teachers' names. Be plugged into their everyday life.
- Introduce your new family to your coworkers.
- Display your family to others—be proud of them all.
- Have fun together. Do things everyone in the family likes to do, not just what you want to do.

## Strong Communication Skills

Communication is vital to bring success in every area of our life. There is an interesting story in Genesis that shows the power that can be attained when good communication meets a common vision:

> *Now the whole world had one language and a common speech. As men moved eastward, they found a plain in Shinar (Babylonia) and settled there. They said to each other, "Come, let's make bricks and bake them thoroughly." They used brick instead of stone, and tar for mortar. Then they said, "Come, let us build ourselves a city, with a tower that reaches to the heavens, so that we may make a name for ourselves and not be scattered over the face of the whole earth." But the Lord came down to see the city and the tower that the men were building. The Lord said, "If as one people speaking the same language they have begun to do this, then nothing they plan to do will be impossible for them"* (Genesis 11:1–6).

Just think about that last sentence. When you and your spouse speak the same language (which I am sure you do), develop common goals, are determined to do whatever it takes to build your new family, and include God's awesome Holy Spirit living inside you as your guide, you *will* succeed.

Although Paige and I have been married since 1989, we still have breakdowns in our communication with each other. I do not mean arguments, but just misunderstandings due to lack of or inadequate communication. When we do not take the time to talk to each other about what is going on, what needs to be done, or when something is bothering us, our relationship and family can become strained.

In Chapter 2 we discussed the fact that husbands and wives will have successful relationships when they work as a team. A vital part of teamwork is communication. Communication is both speaking our thoughts and listening to understand our partner.

In order to have a strong marriage and family, we need to communicate daily, and on many levels in order to:

- express love and appreciation for each other, encouraging each other,
- share goals and dreams,
- understand each other's thoughts and feelings,
- resolve issues within the family,
- discuss and settle business or financial issues, and
- many other reasons.

When communication breaks down or does not exist, assumptions and presumptions will arise. This begins a chain reaction of making decisions without regard to our partner's input, which in turn creates hurt feelings and possible damaged relationships.

Good communication is an art of relaying a message in a way that the listener understands our words and our intent. Yet, many people do not know how to communicate. Perhaps you grew up in a home with poor communication, never learned communication skills, or just do not like to communicate.

There are three main components in spoken communication—our words, our tone of voice, and our body language. A study on communications discovered that of any message we are delivering, only seven percent is our words. Our tone of voice speaks thirty-eight percent of our message, and our non-verbal body language communicates fifty-five percent of our message.

To become a good communicator, we really need to become aware of our tone of voice and body language.

It is not too late to develop great communication in your marriage and with your children. There are many communication skills resources available. The best we have found is, *Collaborative Marriage Skills* by Interpersonal Communication Programs, Inc. Visit www.couplecommunication.com.

## Silence

It is worth repeating part of our discussion from "In the Heat of Battle," found in Chapter 2, about not causing hurt feelings by speaking harsh words when our emotions are high. Emotions can run high on occasions in any relationship, and people often say things they later regret.

> *My dear brothers, take note of this: everyone should be quick to listen, slow to speak and slow to get angry, for man's anger does not bring about the righteous life that God desires* (James 1:19–20).

I would be embarrassed to count how many times I jumped to wrong conclusions about a situation with Paige or one of our children, usually before I had all of the facts, and as a result passed "erred" judgment. I reacted before I should have, creating hurt feelings, lack of respect, and embarrassment. I learned the hard way that it can be good—very good—to just shut up and listen.

> *The tongue has the power of life and death, and those who love it will eat its fruit* (Proverbs 18:21).

What you speak to your spouse will bring life or death to your marriage. What you speak to your children and new children will bring life or death to the relationships you are trying to build with them.

> *With the tongue we praise our Lord and Father, and with it we curse men who have been made in God's likeness Out of the same mouth come praise and cursing. My brothers, this should not be. Can both fresh water and salt water flow from the same spring?* (James 3:9–11).

When your emotions run high, do not speak or react hastily. Calm down before an issue is discussed any further. As the saying goes, "Never miss an opportunity to shut up."

## Listen

An important step during silence is to listen—really listen. Most people are poor listeners. Many would rather be heard than to hear what others have to say. We have an agenda and we want to complete it. When someone disagrees with us, we usually listen to them until they say something that justifies our agenda and we cut them off and reinforce our case.

In good communication, listening involves a different focus. Proper listening has the intent to:

- learn more facts about the issue,
- find out the other person's point of view,
- discover the other person's feelings,
- learn where our presumptions were wrong, and
- develop a solution that is acceptable to both.

Listening has the powerful ability to let the person speaking know that they are important and valued; it will grow the relationship.

## High Grace

God has been so gracious toward you and me. Even before we knew God (or even wanted to know God), He gave to us His Son, who came to serve us and die for our sins that we might live an eternal life in heaven with Father God, as well as an abundant life here. God's forgiveness is available to us every day.

> *If we confess our sins, He is faithful and just to forgive us our sins and to cleanse us from all unrighteousness* (1John 1:9).

Jesus intercedes for us everyday.

> *Who is he who condemns? It is Christ who died, and furthermore is also risen, who is even at the right hand of God, who also makes intercession for us* (Romans 8:34).

What does God expect of us in return for what He has done and continues to do for us? He gave us two commands in the New Covenant:

1. Love God fully.
2. Love others with the same passion that we love ourselves, forgiving others for offenses against us, and extending grace to them.

In Matthew 18:23–30, Jesus told the parable of the unmerciful servant. To summarize the parable, the servant owed the king a huge debt that he was unable to pay. The servant asked the king for mercy (no prison time), and the king completely forgave the servant of his debt. Yet, after being forgiven such a huge debt, the servant went to a man who owed him a much smaller debt and demanded payment. When the man could not pay and asked for mercy, the servant had the man put in prison.

We can often act like the unmerciful servant. Jesus came as the Lamb of God to take away the sins of the world—your sins and my sins. This was a debt that we were unable to pay on our own. Jesus said, "I will pay it!" and He died for our sins. We have been completely forgiven by Father God so generously and so many times.

Yet we may get angry, get offended, or hold a grudge against someone who hurts us, refusing to forgive them. We object when things are not done the way we want. We get angry with someone when they make a mistake or take advantage of us. We may put demands on people, or discipline our children over small, often insignificant things.

One day a coworker and I were talking about rules we had established in our homes. During the course of the conversation, though I disagreed with his permissive parenting style, I realized that many of my rules and expectations for my children were over minor issues (my pet peeves of life). I felt the tug of God urging me to examine the rules and expectations I had established for relatively insignificant things in our family. God began to change my heart, and I made effort to become more gracious toward my family.

Sometimes our biggest expectations of other people are over relatively small things.

"Close the cabinets."

"Clean up your room."

"Turn the lights off when you leave the room."

"Quit drinking milk from the carton."

"For the fourth time, go put the garbage out."

I am not saying that some of these expectations are wrong. I believe we should be respectful of each other, and train our children to handle responsibilities by giving them chores around the home to help keep the home orderly. Responsibilities with consequences when the responsibilities are not completed as agreed are healthy training tools.

I am trying to heighten awareness that, in perspective, such small things have potential to generate anger and harsh tones, adding stress and strife to the family relationships.

Walk in grace. Treat people, including your spouse and children, as you want God to treat you when you have messed up. Don't miss any opportunity to show grace to your family—your entire family. Learn to set other people free from your petty expectations of them. This is grace! Remember, true grace is all-inclusive; it does not exclude anyone.

We should also not miss opportunities to praise and encourage one another in our home.

> *Therefore encourage one another and build each other up, just as in fact you are doing* (1Thessalonians 5:11).

Look for the positive traits and actions in others, and acknowledge them often.

## A Life of Forgiveness

God created man and woman to be in a covenant marriage relationship for a lifetime, as well as to live in peace with their neighbors. Relationships are a very high priority to God. All Ten Commandments given to Moses are about relationships—the first four are about our relationship with God, and the next six are about staying in relationship with each other. All aspects of your life are important to God (your finances, transportation, home, health, etc), but none are more important to God than your relationships.

Yet, God knew that men and women were imperfect and would hurt and offend each other. Therefore, when Jesus came to bring us the New Covenant, He declared that the two most important commandments were:

1. Love God.
2. Love your neighbor as yourself.

In Mosaic Law, if someone hurt, offended, or killed another person, it was an eye for an eye, a tooth for a tooth, and a life for a life. With the New Covenant of His Blood, Jesus changed the rules of forgiveness. The New Covenant requires us to love and do good, even to our enemies (those who hurt, interfere, or in other ways oppose us). Forgiveness is so important to God that He made it a prerequisite for us to receive forgiveness from God.

As we mentioned above, Jesus tells the story of the unmerciful servant—a man who was forgiven so much by his master, but then refused to forgive another. The servant was later thrown into prison for his unwillingness to forgive.

Likewise, God has forgiven our debt that we could not pay. Yet, when we refuse to forgive, we hold others accountable for their actions.

> *Forgive us our debts, as we also have forgiven our debtors. And lead us not into temptation, but deliver us from the evil one. For if you forgive men when they sin against you, your heavenly Father will also forgive you. But if you do not forgive men their sins, your Father will not forgive your sins* (Matthew 6:12–15).

A measure of the true unconditional love we have for someone is when we do not keep a record of wrongs.

... *it [love] keeps no record of wrongs* (1Corinthians 13:5b).

Wouldn't that be a great place to live! Our personal world would be so different if people kept no record of wrongs. Our relationships would thrive if we would stop distancing ourselves from others, or stop bringing up past mistakes and past hurts to each other. I am certain that is how you want others to treat you. But do you treat others that way? Do you walk in forgiveness?

## Steps to Forgiveness

I believe each of us have struggled with forgiveness at some time in our life. I have noticed that people respond to hurts and offenses in one of three ways:

1. Avoidance: We make a decision to distance ourselves from the one who has hurt us. Perhaps you have heard the comment, "With friends like that, who needs enemies?" So we break off the relationship with that person.
2. Tolerance: Perhaps out of necessity we develop a coping skill to establish a casual, shallow relationship with the one who hurt us. Tolerance is common among troublesome family members. (We always need to forgive those who hurt us, but setting boundaries may become necessary to protect ourselves and our family.)
3. Forgiveness: We release the one who hurt us, expecting nothing from them—not even an apology. Our sin separated us from God. The forgiveness God offered us through Jesus Christ restores us back into the presence of Father God. Forgiveness goes far beyond

tolerance, and can provide opportunity for the relationship to be restored and continue to grow. It is important for every relationship to last, but it is even more vital for the covenant of marriage to flourish.

Take a moment to inventory the strained relationships in your life. Make a list of them. For each, note whether you are living a life of avoidance, tolerance, or true forgiveness. If you have unforgiveness toward anyone, realize that it is having a negative affect on your other relationships.

If you have unforgiveness toward your spouse, holding on to it will eventually end your marriage and family. Not forgiving family members, coworkers, or others who have hurt you will negatively affect all of your relationships. Make it your goal to be a follower of Christ and to extend the forgiveness you have received.

The process of forgiveness begins with each of us changing our thoughts, which in turn changes our hearts. The following steps will help you live a forgiving and free life:

1. Recognize that forgiveness is a process, it is not easy, it will take time, and the Holy Spirit will help you. When God requires something of us, He helps us accomplish it.
2. Define the hurt that is causing your unforgiveness. It may be the result of something that happened recently, or even long ago when you were a child. If you cannot determine the cause yourself, consider talking to a pastor or professional counselor. An objective viewpoint can likely help you uncover your source of hurt, frustration or fear.
3. Try to understand the one who has offended you. *We judge our-*

*selves by our intentions, but we judge the one who hurt us by their actions.*

When we have hurt someone, we ask for forgiveness, saying that we did not mean to hurt them; our intentions were right.

However, when someone has hurt us, their actions speak louder than their reasoning, and we usually hold them accountable. We often distance ourselves from the offender.

4. Realize that hurting people will hurt people. Perhaps the one who offended you never intended to harm you the way they have, or maybe the presence of hurt in that person's life causes them to hurt you and others.
5. Seek to see your offender as God sees them. This will happen as you begin to pray for that person. When you hold unforgiveness toward someone, you do not see the value in that person, and you do not want to let them off the hook. Yet, God loves that person as much as He loves you. Jesus paid a great price to remove your sins, and your offender's sins.
6. Separate the offense from the person. When someone has hurt you, every time you see or think of that person you are reminded of that hurt. You tie the hurt from a person to that person.

*For as high as the heavens are above the earth, so great is his love for those who fear him; as far as the east is from the west, so far has he removed our transgressions from us* (Psalm 103:11–12).

When we repent God separates our sin from us. With our sins removed, God only sees our great potential since we are made in His image and likeness. In the same manner that God separates us from our sin, we need to separate the offense from the person who offended us. Good people do bad things, and everyone makes mistakes.

7. Put your feelings in writing. There are two particularly effective ways you can maintain your lifestyle of forgiving and freedom. First, keep a journal or diary, expressing your feelings to God. Do not be afraid to tell God exactly how you are feeling or hurting—He already knows your heart. Writing it down has a way of bringing clarity and healing to you.

   Second, consider writing a letter to the one you have not forgiven. Spell out the offense, and end with a statement of forgiveness and release. Caution: You may or may not choose to deliver the letter. If the other person has negative emotions, he or she will likely not read your letter with the same understanding in which you wrote it. Ask the Holy Spirit to direct your steps.
8. Do something. Loving and staying in relationship requires action.

   *You have heard that it was said, "Love your neighbor and hate your enemy." But I tell you: Love your enemies, bless those who curse you, do good to those who hate you and pray for those who persecute you, that you may be sons of your Father in heaven* (Matthew 5:43–45).

   - Stop talking, slandering, and gossiping about that person.
   - Pray salvation and blessings for your offender. Ask God to help you see them as He sees them, and to love them as He loves them.
   - Do good. Reach out to your offender. Ask God to create such an opportunity.

     —If possible, go to the person,

—If possible re-establish an amicable relationship,

—Apologize for harsh words, or for your part in a damaged relationship.

- Be obedient to Matthew 5:43–45.

9. Allow yourself to grieve your hurt, loss or disappointment. Find a trusted friend to talk to. Allow yourself to cry. Be honest with yourself about any wrong actions or reactions you added in your relationship.
10. Look forward.

*For I know the thoughts that I think toward you, says the LORD, thoughts of peace and not of evil, to give you a future and a hope (Jeremiah 29:11).*

God speaks only of and plans for your future—never your past or your present. After you have grieved, learn from your past and quit looking back. Move forward.

11. Exercise. Find a friend this week and let the other person represent the one who you have not forgiven. Look them in the eye and release them in the following manner:

"I do not know why you _____ (describe how the person hurt you) _____, but it hurt me deeply. I am tired of thinking negative thoughts when I think of you—it drains the life out of me each time I do. Today I put this behind me. I choose to forgive you even though you did not ask for forgiveness. I release you from any payback. You owe me nothing. I expect nothing from you, not even an apology. I ask God to bless you in a way that only He can. I ask the Holy Spirit to seal my forgiveness with

His love and power. From this day forward I vow to walk in His love toward you, and to keep no record of wrongs, in honor and obedience to God's Word."

Do this exercise for each person you have not forgiven, repeating it daily until the harsh feelings leave—you will feel a release in your soul.

## New Family Traditions

Think back and recall some of the things that made your family special when you were growing up. It may have been how you celebrated birthdays, spent a summer with grandma, a special meal shared by your entire family on a certain holiday, or an annual summer vacation that evolved into a family reunion as your family grew older.

For several consecutive years, my family held a three-day family reunion at the same hotel on the Mississippi Gulf Coast. Every Thanksgiving my mom roasted a turkey with special meat dressing, and every Christmas she cooked a large pot of chicken and smoked sausage gumbo with rice and potato salad.

Paige's holiday traditions were quite different from mine. Her family always took out the best china to serve Thanksgiving and Christmas dinners. They spent every Christmas Eve at the Bonfire Festival along the Mississippi River in Gramercy, Louisiana. For many years her mom made banana nut bread to give out as gifts at Christmas time.

## God Established Traditions for His People

God established several annual festivals for the Jewish people in the Old Testament so the Jews would not forget what God had done for them. The Passover feast is an annual celebration in remembrance of the time God spared the lives of first-born Jewish sons when they were in slavery in Egypt under Pharaoh. Through this festival, the Jews remember who their God is and what He did for them and their nation when He freed them from slavery and captivity.

Other memorial Jewish celebrations included the Feast of Weeks and the Feast of Tabernacles. There is much significance tied to each part of those annual celebrations, focusing on the relationship between God and the Jewish nation.

## Traditions Define Your Family

Every major city in the world is made unique by special traditions, events, or monuments that were founded in each city. Washington, D.C. is known as the U.S. Government seat. People vacation in D.C. to visit significant landmarks such as the White House, the Capitol, the Smithsonian Institute museums, and many other historical buildings and monuments.

Calgary, Canada is known as the host city of the 1988 Winter Olympics.

New York City is famous for Broadway, Wall Street, the Statue of Liberty, the New York Yankees and New York Mets baseball teams, and Ground Zero.

Destin, Florida is known for its white sand beaches and fun-in-the-sun.

In a similar way, family traditions *define* your family. They make your family unique, special, and fun. And they will hold a special place in your family members' hearts for the rest of their lives.

Usually, it is a blend of the traditions from you and your spouse's childhood families that is carried into your new family. Every year since we married, Paige bakes several loaves of banana-nut bread (like her Mom did) between Thanksgiving and Christmas, wraps them in aluminum foil and puts them in the freezer. As needed, we pull them out to take to parties, to bless some friends or to share as a snack with co-workers.

Often when a family experiences divorce or death of a spouse, everything changes, including traditions of that family. Trying to carry the same family traditions of your former marriage into your new home can produce painful memories of the broken relationship, and doing this fails to make your new family unique and special.

Because of this, we suggest modifying or abandoning former traditions, and creating new traditions that will define your new family. It is important to establish new traditions to identify the newness and uniqueness of your family. They will make your children feel they belong to a special family, and will enhance the enjoyment of belonging to your family.

Here are some examples of some new family traditions that our family and other families have developed:

1. We have our Thanksgiving dinner on the Friday after Thanksgiving each year.
2. One family shared: "On the first Saturday morning of December, we drive to a small-town bakery a few miles away. This bakery is known for its exquisite gingerbread men. They're soft and chewy, and these fellows are big, almost eight inches tall! We buy several dozen of them; once home, we place them in our holiday cookie bowl. From that moment on, all rules about 'saving dessert for last' are ignored. Anyone can have a gingerbread man at any time,

without asking, throughout the rest of the month! We eat gingerbread men for breakfast, enjoy them while we make decorations, offer them to our friends when visiting, give them to delivery people when packages and letters arrive, and nibble them when we watch our favorite movies.

"If we begin to run out of gingerbread men, we take another trip to the bakery and replenish our supply; the bowl is never empty. This bowl, filled with an endless supply of sweetness, encourages us to practice generosity not only to our friends and visitors, but also toward each other, and to ourselves."

3. During Christmas season when our children were young, Paige and I let our children secretly pick each other's names in our family (known in Louisiana as Kris Kringle). Then we would take a trip to Walmart or Target to let them buy their $5 gifts. It was always fun watching them avoid each other in the store as they made their selections. They exchanged the gifts on Christmas Eve, Christmas Day, or the next time our family was together. This tradition continues today among our grown children. They now mail their gifts to each other across the nation.
4. When preparing a special holiday dinner, make each child's favorite dish. That way, each child will know they were thought about when you prepared the family dinner. (Most dishes can be prepared and frozen ahead of time.)

## The Holiday Juggle

Establishing new traditions around holidays can be difficult since your children may now have more family events to attend (with up to two sets of parents and four sets of grandparents), but it is not impossible.

Special holidays become more than a challenge—often resulting in a competition with one or more former spouses to have all children with them for Christmas, or Easter, or Thanksgiving. During the holidays it is time to use your imagination, be flexible, and turn an unpleasant situation to your advantage.

Need an example? Christmas does not have to fall on December 25 if you cannot get all of your family members together on that day. You can have Christmas dinner and open presents a few days earlier or later. Having all of your new family together is what's important. Besides, opening presents a few days earlier or later makes the holiday last longer.

Do not let former spouses or circumstances altar your attitude. As needed, be flexible and work around other's plans for the betterment of your family. Palm trees growing near the ocean shores can weather hurricanes because God designed them to be extremely flexible. Likewise, you will weather the storms and struggles in life best through developing a flexible attitude.

## Finances for Blended Families

We are not financial planners, and we do not profess to be financial experts. But we do know that financial disagreements and poor financial planning have caused many marriage problems and have destroyed some marriages. We know that Blended Families have unique financial issues that they may face, including child support, one or two bank accounts, alimony payments, court costs, decisions about private or public school, and whether both biological parents will help pay for the children's education.

Here are some general considerations about Blended Family finances:

1. Child support is mandated by the courts, and biological parents should be willing to provide for the needs of their children. Child support should be used for the intended children and should not be considered part of the household income. Use your common sense and follow your heart when deciding where child support should be spent. If there is more child support than is needed for the children to live, a savings account for future educational or other expenses should be considered.

   Considering child support part of your household income will catch up with you. Child support can increase or decrease, and will eventually stop. As an example, in the State of Louisiana child support ends when the child turns eighteen.

   If you are paying child support, we know that you have no control of how the money is spent, or whether it is spent on the children. Our advice is to forgive, release, and hold no grudge toward the parent receiving the support. Pray for that parent, and ask God to bless the money you are sending to bring glory to His Name. Any other attitude is destructive to you and your marriage.
2. Other than child support, any other resources that a parent wants to voluntarily direct to his or her biological children should only be done in a joint decision with his or her new spouse. This is called "respect," and demonstrates the priority relationship deserving of the new spouse.
3. Favoritism should be avoided when spending money on children in your home for gifts, sports, and other extracurricular activities. In our home, each child was allowed to participate in one sport at

a time. For Christmas and birthdays the same amount of money was spent on each child. When planning a family vacation, pick an affordable venue so that everyone can participate.

4. As we discussed in Chapter 2, Genesis 2:24 says that husband and wife are to work to become "one." A husband and wife may have agreed to have two bank accounts, but they should realize that dividing their finances is counterproductive to becoming one. Two bank accounts is possibly a symptom of wanting to maintain independence, a lack of trust, or a lack of respect toward each other. A successful, love-filled marriage is an interdependent relationship between two people; it is not two independent people living together.

## A Positive Attitude

Attitudes are contagious. Just hang around a complaining person and you will become a complainer. If your best friend is a gossip, you may have also become one. Fill your mind with the daily news and the quantity of bad news will make you fearful and oppressed. Continual negative reinforcement will have a negative affect on your attitude.

It is so important for spouses to develop a positive atmosphere in the new home. This positive atmosphere starts with how each spouse interacts and responds to each family member. Just as a church congregation takes on the heart of the pastor, the family members will eventually mimic the heart of the parents.

Always respond—never react. A negative reaction to a negative situation will prevent a successful resolution to the problem, and will create hurt feelings and instability. An appropriate, positive response to negative situations will bring healing and stability.

Realize that the attitudes you see your children or new children display may come from negative words or actions they have experienced from many sources—including from children or workers at a daycare center, behavior of peers at school, a program on television, violence on video games, anger from the other biological parent, a classmate struggling with his or her home life, something they overheard inside your new home, the way he or she is treated in your new home, and such. (We further discuss the children in Chapter 5.)

## Action Steps

- Take a self-assessment and determine if you are individually whole. Review the Mirror-Mirror on the Wall in Appendix B, and be honest with yourself. If needed, seek out appropriate self-help resources for divorce recovery, grief recovery, anger management, or get personal Christian counseling.
- If your children (of any age) have overheard you and your spouse arguing, fighting, or yelling, stop it now, and apologize to each child for any additional pain you may have created in their hearts.
- Establish a high standard of righteousness and excellence in your home. Set goals to achieve that standard, and identify obstacles that hinder the accomplishment of those goals.
- Review the list of proper order above, and develop goals to change any lack of order that exists in your home.
- Determine ways that you can give of yourself to your new family—specific acts for each individual. Then do them, and continue to be a giver in your family.
- Think of ways you can extend grace to your new family mem-

bers, especially toward the ones with whom you seem to be having trouble in developing relationship.

- This year start one new family tradition that you will repeat each year.
- Be flexible when working out a holiday visitation schedule, and take the pressure off of yourself and the children.
- Write down ten positive thoughts about your new family. Repeat this often.

## Our Prayer for You

Father, we ask You to help each spouse to devote the time needed to become individually whole through You.

Help this couple to see the need and to establish God's order in their home so that the home is built on Your foundation. As they raise the standard, increase their faith that You will cause their family to prosper.

Teach this new family to walk in Your incredible grace—pardoning the hurts from others. Pierce their hearts with a fresh love and respect for each other. Give them the courage to wash every member of their new family with acts of love, extending much mercy and grace toward every person.

Thank You for always being there when they need You most. We love You Lord.

We thank You, Jesus. Amen.

## Funny Family Moments

On our winter vacation to Indianapolis, there was ten inches of snow covering the ground. Granddad borrowed some snow sleds from neighbors and we found a schoolyard with a hill that sloped down into a parking lot. We snow-sled for two hours and had a blast. We took turns soloing, in pairs, with two sleds hooked together, going backwards, and each time laughing from the top to the bottom of the hill—until Moe, who was sliding in a plastic sled, hit a drain grate sticking up in the parking lot. Ouch! His tailbone hurt for twelve months.

## Chapter 6

# The Children's Perspective

### *Moe Becnel*

*I feel growing up was different for me than for the rest of the kids in our family. Although our oldest sister had moved out already, the remaining three kids, not including myself, all lived together in Baton Rouge while I finished high school and continued to live with my other set of parents in another state. For me, it was hard to live two lives, so to speak. I had my family, school, friends and job in one state, while traveling back to another state on the weekends to spend time with family and still make time for friend-visits there.*

*Still today, I feel like I am missing something that the other kids share. As the youngest of five, I have always realized every sibling, whether two years or ten years apart, were all at different phases in life. Of course we love each other just the same, but because of the physical distance, the brother-sister or sister-sister or parent-daughter bonds never really seemed to sink in.* —Jessica

*All I feel like I know to say about the children's perspective is that divorce will be experienced a little differently by every child in the family, because every child is different. For example, I automatically assumed a role where I would look out for my younger sister, which*

*is something I still do to this day. (It has partly shaped the kind of person I've become.)*

*So for me, it was kind of like a "You need to grow up real fast . . . your sister needs you" kind of thing. (No one told me this . . . it's just something that clicked inside of me.)*

*I doubt my sister was thinking anything similar to that at the time of the divorce. She was probably just thinking, "Where's my dad . . . and why did he leave?"* —Nicole

*"Two Christmases—more presents!" That was my feeble attempt at a joke. The divorce I experienced was one of strain and hurt. The things I remember most in my early childhood included a custody battle, religious differences, longing for acceptance by my two new stepsisters who had a biological bond between them, feelings of exclusion by my dad's new family, and general awkwardness about relationships—do I call my step-dad "Dad"?*

*Looking back, having to navigate through all this left me with a serious identity crisis—although I didn't know it at the time. This continued through my adolescent and early adulthood years.*

▪ ▪ ▪

THE *ITALICIZED COMMENTS* in this chapter are from our daughter Nicole Duplechain, who teaches the Children's Perspective class of the Reach for Recovery (divorce recovery) curriculum at Healing Place Church. The italicized comments are her personal thoughts from the perspective of a child of divorce.

## Preparation

We want to prepare you for the content and purpose of this chapter. The Children's Perspective is not about you; it is about and for the children in your new family. We are advocates for the children whose lives have been adversely changed by the death of a parent or by adult decisions (such as divorce). Read it for them, to understand what they may be thinking and how they may be feeling. Read it to determine how you can become their advocate.

Although the material in this chapter is eye-opening and rather blunt, it can greatly help you to help all the children in your world—yours, your spouse's, and others.

There is no blame or guilt here. If you begin feeling either guilt or blame, remember the grace and forgiveness Father God lavishes on you when you repent.

## The Children's Experience

Children in a Blended Family almost always come from a past of brokenness, either from the death of a parent or from divorce. They have suffered deep loss and deep hurts that they did not deserve; some of those hurts and the consequences of the loss continue in their lives for many years.

As we stated before, God hates divorce because it rips people apart, and wounds them for years to come.

*Twenty one years later, the divorce still affects my planning. When planning a family function like a birthday party, I try to think how it can be done where everyone (parents, grandparents, other extended family, siblings from both families, etc.) feels comfortable. —Nicole*

As we said in an earlier chapter, when children are involved, divorce or death of a spouse is the death of a small civilization. The broken civilization fractures the future of the people involved; their visions, dreams and plans crumble, at least for a season, and create wounded people and strained lifestyles.

Children of divorce are innocent victims who are propelled into brokenness by at least one of their parents. The children are often caught within a battle of selfishness, having to deal with angry parents, at times getting put in the middle, and getting repeatedly wounded.

Here are common things children struggle with:

- Many children were shocked by the announcement that their parents were divorcing. They did not see it coming, or they did not think the issues between Mom and Dad were serious. In some cases, the parents pretended all was fine until the announcement came. I heard one child say, "I never heard my parents argue."
- The children's world and dreams become shattered.
- They often hear parents speak negatively of each other, reopening the wounds.
- Many feel rejected or even abandoned by one of their parents. Many think they are not loved.
- The child who had one parent leave may fear the domicile parent will also leave.
- Some are frequently used as a communication tool, so the non-communicating parents can avoid speaking to each other.
- These children often live a life of travel or distance living—they are the ones packing the bags and commuting to the other home every week, every other weekend, or whatever the courts have arranged.

- Some young children living in a single-parent home are given too much responsibility for their age, and then are punished or feel guilty when they fail.
- Children of divorce and children whose parent has died both go through a similar grieving process, grieving loss.
- A broken home means insecurity and instability as they adjust to two homes and changing environments.

As an adult goes through divorce or death of a spouse, their children go with them.

*Young children need to know that their mom and dad have their hand in life. If they do not feel that, the children will believe "I cause their (the parents) weakness." —Nicole*

Because the parents are dealing with their own pain, the child's pain is often overlooked. And at a time when hurting widowed, separated, or divorced parents seem least able to properly parent, parental roles increase. Some of the new demands include:

- becoming Mom & Dad in the domicile home,
- focusing on all of the financial, educational, medical, transportation, recreational, and household needs of the single parent family, and
- trying to be sensitive to the children's feelings, emotions, actions, reactions.

Parents have another vital role—helping the children heal, and showing the children that their future is bright with God. Oftentimes, children do not tell parents how they are feeling.

*Children often do not really know how they feel. When my parents divorced, I did not know if I felt sadness, or anger, or disbelief, or if I was afraid. I was kindof numb. And I felt different at the ages of seven, seventeen and twenty-seven (and all the ages in between). —Nicole*

Because of the mega-thousands of divorces, we now have a generation of children in pain. This is evident by the increase of gangs, the high level of violence in schools and the rise in teen suicide today—all caused by kids who are hurting. Like many adults, children use anger and aggression to hide their pain.

You will hear us make the following statement several times in this book: *Hurting people hurt other people, and hurting people are also easily hurt again.* Where there is heat (anger), there is hurt. If children are angry, they will create hurt in other people's lives.

## How Children of Broken Homes Think and Feel

Sherry May, Children's Pastor at Healing Place Church, has worked with many children who live with broken homes and broken hearts. We met with her to find out how these children express themselves. Here are a few questions, comments and thoughts that some of the children have verbalized to her:

- "My dad left home because he did not love me enough to stay."
- Parents do not try hard enough to reconcile. "Why don't they (my parents) try one more time?"
- "I feel responsible for the divorce. It was my fault."
- "They argue about me."
- "Why are they mad at me?"
- "When will my mom stop hating my dad?" "When will my dad stop hating my mom?" *Even adult children feel that way; that question never ends as long as there is strife. —Nicole*

- "Why did they divorce?"
- "No one asks me how I am feeling." "I am waiting for someone to ask me if I am okay."
- "When will I stop hurting?"
- "Why do I have to be the 'go-between'?"

Note the frequency of comments above in which a child takes the blame for the divorce. This is the perception of many children.

As a result of the loss and pain, children's lives may become chaotic, marked by multiple emotional swings of anger, sadness, numbness, regret, blame, guilt, fear, and sorrow. As these emotions rise up, children may exhibit a variety of dysfunctional behaviors in response to their conflicted emotions. The most common negative behaviors include poor grades in school, disrespect toward parents or other adults, lack of trust in other people (especially adults), isolation, verbal anger, oppression, depression, and involvement with the wrong crowd.

Until their hurts are healed, children will carry negative thoughts and emotions for years, and as Nicole stated, will re-process the loss and subsequent pain at various ages in their life.

At the beginning of this chapter and elsewhere in the book, you read comments from the hearts of some of our children. Every child has a different story—no two children or situations are alike. Yet all children who have experienced divorce or loss of a parent have these things in common:

- They do not have much to celebrate.
- They must have hope.
- They must have healing.
- They need to experience true, unconditional love.

- They long for acceptance from all new family members.
- They need security and stability to be reestablished, which produces confidence in their lives.
- They need a peaceful, loving environment to be reestablished.
- They need a solid, loving family as a role model for their future.
- They need the cycle of divorce to be broken in their lives.

Everyone needs hope and healing in his or her life. Even King David, a man after God's own heart, needed hope and healing. David declared,

> *I am still confident of this: I will see the goodness of the Lord in the land of the living* (Psalm 27:13).

It is apparent to me that there was not much good in David's life at the time he wrote that verse.

## Hurting People Hurt People

Just like their parents, hurting children need restoration in their lives.

*Hurting people hurt other people, and hurting people are easily hurt (again) by other people. —Nicole*

We all know people, adults and children alike, who walk through each day angry or disappointed with other people in their life. They go through life with a "pocket full of rocks," ready to hurt others or defend themselves. They keep walls up to protect their hearts from being hurt again.

These same people are easily offended. I am sure you know someone like that. You have to "walk on egg shells" around him or her because you don't know when you might say or do something that will cause an emotional outburst.

Understanding the fact that hurting people hurt people has helped me to properly respond to hurts from other people. I now understand that their hurtful comments or actions are due to pain they are dealing with, and not necessarily or completely directed at me. This understanding helps me to not react negatively or take offense.

*But healed people heal other people. —Nicole*

When we have forgiven our offenders and find our individual wholeness, we are able to help hurting people. This is our role as parents in the new family we are building. Both parents and new parents have the ability and responsibility to love, care for, provide for, defend, teach, and guide their children. God wants to use both of you as the instrument of His hope and healing in the lives of your new family—to help each of them find healing from past hurts.

*This is hard to do if the child is hurting from the other parent. Teach them to forgive—show them how to forgive. —Nicole*

We end this section with this quote:

> "Never underestimate the power of dreams and the influence
> of the human spirit. We are all the same in this notion.
> The potential for greatness lives within each of us."
> —Wilma Rudolph, 1960 Olympic Medalist

As you heal and find your new dreams in life, help your children find their healing and their new dreams. The human spirit is strong when it is encouraged to press on. You are the catalyst for the children in your world to reach their God-given potential.

## Do's & Don'ts to Help Hurting Children

1. *Do* communicate with your children. Ask them how they are feeling. Be concerned for their hurting heart. Ask them what they may have overheard their parents say that deeply hurt or troubled them. Allow your children to vent and express themselves without reacting negatively. Maintain respect for each other.
2. *Do* use the team of people available to you. Oftentimes a child will not talk to their parents because they are insecure and they fear hurting, angry, or alienating their parent. In the case of divorce, they may fear the domicile parent will leave them also.

   Identify your team; utilize close friends, teachers, pastors, or counselors to help your child vent and talk through their pain. A third party can often bring clarity and a new perspective to your child.
3. *Do* tell the children that the divorce was not their fault. It was an adult choice.
4. *Do* affirm the children. They are not mistakes of the marriage that ended.
5. *Do* tell them that God hates divorce, but God loves people who have been through divorce.
6. *Do* tell the children they must face the truth. When people live in denial, they carry more baggage and carry it longer.
7. *Do* allow the children to grieve. Do not tell them to "Get over it." Periodically encourage them to express their heart, to talk about their feelings. One of the laws of motion is, "What goes up must come down." The Law of Emotion is, "What we push down (suppress) will eventually come up."
8. *Do* become the children's support. Provide for them spiritually,

physically, and emotionally.

9. *Do* be consistent in your life—your rules, discipline, and time with them.
10. *Do* pursue your own complete healing. As stated before, if you are not healthy, your children will not be healthy. If you have anger, they will pick it up. *Let God undo the layers of hurt and unforgiveness in your heart. You will either build on top of your unforgiveness, or you can let God heal you. You will then be able to help your children heal. —Nicole*
11. *Do* show them how to heal and accept their new life, as you obtain your healing.
12. *Do* apologize to them for the hurts in their life. (An apology is so important that we will repeat this in the book.)
13. *Do* ask them to forgive you for any hurts you may have caused.
14. *Do* teach your children how to forgive. Help them unload the rocks in their pockets—the unforgiveness and anger they have toward other people. Forgiveness says, "I release you and expect nothing from you, not even an apology."
15. *Do* model what you want to see. Your children will do what you do. Let your life match your words. Watch what you are saying and doing. Be cautious of what you expose them to.
16. *Do* help the children set new, realistic dreams and goals, as you (the parent) do the same. Doing this helps you take them with you on your life journey. Caution: Some children are not emotionally ready to move forward when you are. Be patient as they heal.
17. *Do* break the cycle of divorce in your children's lives. Commit to them and to God that you will do your very best to not put them through another divorce.

18. *Do* pray for and with your children every day.
19. *Do* tell them that God still has a good and prosperous plan for their life. Read and explain Jeremiah 29:11 to them.
20. *Do* have fun.
21. *Don't* let the children become your support. This is too much responsibility for many adults, much less your children.
22. *Don't* share adult matters, family matters, or your hurts with your children. *Preserve their innocence. Your bitterness will embitter their hearts. Let them be children. —Nicole*
23. *Don't* overload the children with responsibilities.
24. *Don't* eliminate rules or withhold discipline.
25. *Don't* put the other parent down, or in any way speak negative about them—even where children might overhear you.
26. *Don't* use the children as a pawn, putting them in a difficult place.

Psychological studies have shown that the age of a child at the time of the death of a parent or divorce is reflective of the number of years it takes that child to heal. In other words, if a child was twelve years old when the parents divorced, it could take up to twelve years for that child to heal.

We believe God is bigger than that, and can move mountains in people's lives, including their hurts, in a supernatural way. And God will use biological parents and new parents to be an instrument, a catalyst that will speed up the healing process in the children's lives. Parents have to be intentional in this effort.

## Children in Blended Families

Children entering a Blended Family are forced to deal with several new issues, including instability, acceptance, new rules, new people and personalities, "another" new environment, competition between new siblings, and new authority figures.

Approximately ninety-nine percent of the families we hear from or provide guidance to describe an issue with at least one child in their family. The child is often marked or blamed as a problem in the new family.

There are legitimate reasons for the children's behaviors, but the children are not the cause of conflict. The children are simply reacting to the environment changes that either the death of a parent or the adult decisions of divorce and/or remarriage has created. It is not surprising to us when children respond negatively to again being pushed into a new unstable environment that they did not ask for, a new family with a new parent figure, and possibly new siblings.

As previously divorced or widowed parents, we must be considerate of our children's ongoing disappointments, feelings and struggles. Remember, they did not ask for the breakup of their biological home. They also did not ask for a new Blended Family lifestyle.

## Hesitant to Emotionally Connect

Here is a list of nineteen possible reasons (there are probably more) why a child may resist emotionally connecting to your new Blended Family. We have discussed some of these already, but we list them here to show the magnitude of issues that children can face. As you read these and see one or more that may relate to one of your children, write the child's name next to it. The possible reasons are:

1. The Parent Trap. The fulfillment of a single parent's dream to marry, or remarry, becomes the death of their children's dream to see Mom & Dad reconcile. Some children will intentionally resist the new home and try to sabotage the remarriage to reestablish their dream of Mom and Dad together again.
2. A child may still be hurting and angry from the divorce.
3. A child may be grieving the death of a parent.
4. One or more unhealed, hurting parents are displaying anger, depression, or other mood swings, causing the children in the home to "walk on egg shells."
5. A child fears the pain of another home failing. "The last one failed; this one probably will also," they reason, so they protect their heart by not emotionally connecting.
6. Children are in competition with the new parent for their biological parent's time and attention.
7. There is competition between new siblings in the home.
8. The child senses a betrayal factor—"If I get close to my new dad, I will hurt my real dad, or my real dad will get mad."
9. There is favoritism in the new home created by different rules for different children, or by special attention or privileges or finances given to some. Favoritism is more pronounced in Blended Families due to lack of bonding and parental guilt.
10. A child feels rejection or abandonment from a biological parent who seldom or never contacts them, or who lives a great distance from them, resulting in minimal visitation.
11. A child resents discipline from a new parent who expresses no love toward them.
12. A child does not feel accepted by the new parent, which gener-

ates a feeling of not belonging in the new home. This will cause the child to want to live with their other parent. If the only love a child feels in a home is from their biological parent, the home is divided.

13. The child is hurt from non-acceptance by extended family members.
14. A child hears negative talk from one biological parent who is bitter at the other biological parent.
15. A child is in a "position change" in the new family. For example, an oldest or youngest child in the biological family may no longer be the oldest or youngest in the Blended Family. This can affect a child's emotional identity in the new family (from Helen Wheeler, www.changingfamilies.com).
16. The child's identity has been lost in the new home. For instance, the child's last name may be Stevens, but the domicile home has the last name of Roberts.
17. Teenagers may resist the new family because they may be dealing with many hormones, wanting independence, the new environment, peer pressure, or the breakup of their biological home. Sometimes their resistance is a Blended Family issue; sometimes it is the fact that they are in their teen years. Sometimes the resistance is a combination of both.
18. Some children have seen parents go through many dating and/or marriage relationships, so they have learned to not emotionally attach. They keep their distance to protect their heart from a revolving door of people who come and go from their life.
19. The Blended Family changes their family life forever, adding multiple new family members, which can be overwhelming for many children.

Some children have a difficult time coping with adversity; others do not know what to do with their negative feelings. As Nicole stated earlier, a child may not even know what they are feeling. They have shattered dreams and do not know how to let go of impossible dreams. It is your responsibility as parents to help your children as they reprocess and work through their ever-changing negative feelings.

As long as the issues with which they struggle are left unresolved, these issues will continue to rise up and affect you and your new family, as well as the child's future.

A pastoral counselor or a professional Christian counselor could be very beneficial if those situations linger for several months with no improvement.

We shared this next verse in the last chapter, but we reinforce it here to speak this promise over the lives of your children.

> *The Spirit of the Sovereign Lord is on Me, because the Lord has anointed Me to preach good news to the poor. He has sent Me to bind up the brokenhearted, to proclaim freedom for the captives and release for the prisoners, to proclaim the year of the Lord's favor and the day of vengeance of our God, to comfort all who mourn, and provide for those who grieve in Zion—to bestow on them a crown of beauty instead of ashes, the oil of gladness instead of mourning, and a garment of praise instead of a spirit of despair* (Isaiah 61: 1–3).

Wow! What a gift from heaven God gave to us and our children. Jesus came to do these things for them, too. Our responsibility to our children is to help them tap into that source. We are (or should be) God's hands, feet and voice to our hurting children.

Just one of the above "hesitant to connect" reasons can affect a child's attitude toward their new environment. If a child is feeling emotions from two or more of these nineteen issues, the disconnect will be more pronounced, and will take longer for the child to overcome.

There is long-term effect of a child remaining emotionally disconnected. We have seen such children struggle to make commitments to marriage when they become adults. A child may fear that if Mom and Dad could not be successful in marriage, how will he or she make it? If a child protects their heart for so long by not emotionally connecting to the family, this pattern could easily carry over into their own marriage and family.

With proper guidance and through an unconditional love experience, each child can overcome their hesitancies. In the following sections, we will further discuss some of the key issues children in Blended Families can face, and some steps the adults can take to help the children overcome each.

## Need for Stability

In the last chapter we spoke of the need to create stability in your marriage relationship.

Children whose worlds have been shaken through loss of a parent or through a broken home also need to find stability again. They usually miss their other biological parent as well as their former familiar surroundings, friends, and lifestyle. Their other biological parent may have died; or the parent may live hours away, ignore them, or passively reject them.

The new home may also feel unstable; the children may sense disorganization, or lack of unity. A child may fear that the new family will fall apart and end just as their last family did. As the teenage son of a friend of ours told his mom, "Every time a man leaves you, he leaves me, too." As his mom had struggled with previous marriages and relationships, the teen had experienced multiple people walk in and out of his life. He was protective of attaching his heart again.

Above all, children of divorce need a solid family foundation because they learn and develop character based upon their environment. Your children will mimic you. As they grow up, they will most likely say what you said and do what you did, and may even parent as you have parented them. Your new home should exemplify a strong family, and serve as a positive role model for each child's own future family.

It is the responsibility of the husband and wife to produce a positive, stable atmosphere—built on love, caring, and grace from both parents. Such a home will provide a source of healing for your children.

If the only love the child feels in the new home is from his or her biological parent, the home atmosphere is divided. The child will not feel a part of the new family, and will not find a source of healing from his or her past hurts.

When new parents do not love their new spouse's children and make no effort to do so, the new home will remain fragmented and unstable. Realize that you cannot truly love your spouse without loving his or her children. Remember, your spouse and his or her children were one before the two of you shared vows. If you think of them as non-connected people, you will likely treat them that way. Any conscious or unconscious actions to divide the biological parent/child relationship will usually result in separation of hearts between you and your spouse, and could lead to the deterioration of your marriage (we further discuss this in Chapter 6.).

## Apologies Bring Healing

During the early years of our marriage, our family was not growing, had no peace, and we were struggling to make positive change. I recall one Sunday afternoon when Paige and I gathered our family and sat on our living room floor in a circle. Paige and I apologized to each child for the fact that he or she had been put through a divorce. We told them that divorce was not what we had planned for or wanted in our life, and was certainly not what we wanted for them. We then told them that we wanted our new family to be a loving family, and we wanted to be their parents when they were in our home (we will clarify the roles of new parents in Chapter 6).

We also apologized for all the times we had treated any child unfairly, held a grudge against them, or failed to make them feel a part of our life or of the family. After the apologies, we allowed each child to share what was on his or her heart. Most of the children did not comment but just wept. We cried together, and then prayed for each child. What a breakthrough we had! Our time of apology made a difference in everyone's attitude, and created a kinder, softer respect and appreciation for each other. It was a step in the healing process for each of us, and a definite turning point for our family.

Brian and Jessica are parents of a great Blended Family, which includes Jessica's two young sons. We encouraged them to apologize to her boys as we had done with our children. Later they shared the following story:

The four of them sat down and Mom apologized to her boys for the divorce and any hurts in their heart. Both boys started crying, but her oldest ran into his bedroom. She went in to talk to him, and he asked, "Mom, why did you and Dad have to divorce?" She wanted to spare her boys of the details of the abusive issues in her former marriage, so she said, "Mommy was not listening to God."

He grabbed paper and crayons, and made a card for his mom. It said, "Mommy, listen to God. I love you!" He came back into the living room and gave it to her and hugged her. Jessica told us that his attitude changed from that day forward.

If you have not apologized to your children (or even if you have) for the undeserved pain in their life, we urge you to do it—or do it again. Apologize to your children for the divorce. Do it even if you were not the one who left the former marriage, or you did not intend to produce the hurt in your children, or you did everything to try to reconcile the former marriage.

Your apology may be the only one your children will ever get—and it will be another step in their healing.

## Can I Fix It?

Children see things differently than parents do. In a physical sense, Paige and I have grown children, so our home is no longer "child-proof." As a result, when any of our six young grandchildren are coming over, Paige assesses our home in order to prepare for their visit. Paige will get on her knees and view the room to see what our grandchildren might see, and remove those things that can hurt them or that they can break.

In a perceptive sense, children are also aware of their world—more than we realize, and often more than we hope. Let us share this recent story:

Brian and Jessica recently went through a difficult time. Brian got hurt, had to have two surgeries, and missed three weeks of work. He had insurance, but no sick leave, so he had no salary while he was recovering.

Jessica has two sons who live with them, and whom Brian calls his own, and they have two beautiful daughters together. Bobby, their seven-year-old son, overheard his mom and new dad talking about how tight the household finances were (children overhear a lot—way too much). Bobby told his mom that he wanted to help the family so he painted a picture entitled "Tornado Mixer," and with Brian's help he put it on eBay for auction. The picture—which really was priceless—sold for $50.00.

His parents did not intend to take his money, but Bobby insisted in helping. So Bobby paid $5.00 tithe to his church, $30.00 toward the family electric bill, and he kept $15.00. Wow!

We see these four interesting points in Bobby's story:

1. Bobby was keenly aware of the family's problem—even at age seven.
2. Bobby wanted to be a part of fixing the problem.
3. He came up with his own plan.
4. The picture Bobby painted was of a tornado. This may have symbolized how he saw his world (home) during that time.

Your children are likely aware of problems in your home, or in their life. Children may even feel responsible for the problems, and may likely try to fix them. As we stated before, children frequently blame themselves for the divorce that broke their home.

A child trying to "fix their world" can be both good and bad. In the case of Bobby, it was an event that helped bond their family. Yet, one of the problems that many children of divorce attempt to fix in their world is to getting their biological parents back together, even if it means sabotaging new relationships and remarriages. Hence, *The Parent Trap* movies were created.

## The Parent Trap

You are likely familiar with *The Parent Trap* movies. A couple gets divorced and their children try to get Mom and Dad back together—and will go to great lengths and employ various schemes to make this happen. Hollywood makes it cute and funny, but the reality is that there are children who attempt to fix their world—even after Mom and/or Dad are remarried.

We repeat from earlier, the day you fulfilled your dream to remarry was likely the day your child's dream to see Mom and Dad back together died.

Parents cannot allow their children to undermine their new marriage covenant. The Bible warns us about the seriousness of the marriage covenant in God's eyes.

> *So then, they are no longer two but one flesh Therefore what God has joined together, let not man separate* (Matthew 19:6, Mark 10:9).

This includes not letting your children separate you from your spouse. Stand firm for your marriage. Support your spouse first and foremost. Your children may not understand this now, but they do not need to experience another divorce. They need to experience a family in which the husband and wife honor their covenant with God and with each other, and who live in harmony with each other.

## Action Steps

As described above, your child's desire to fix things can be good and bad, depending on the issue.

- If the situation involves something they can accomplish to help your new family, give them the open door to help. Allowing your child to help will make them feel a vital part of and important to the family.

- If they are trying to fix their world to the detriment of your new marriage, you must intervene to defend your marriage. Be aware. Do not assume your child would not do that.
- Make sure your child does not feel responsible for the divorce, or for the circumstances in their life. Reassure them of this, and of your love for them.
- Ask your child what their dreams are. Get to know what is inside their heart. Help them to let go of unrealistic dreams and build new dreams. Be the catalyst that helps your child develop new dreams. (They may also need to hear from their biological parent that their dreams are not realistic.)
- Apologize to them for the undeserved hurts they have experienced.
- Ask them what they would like to change in their life, or in your family—if it were possible. Do not react to what they say.

## Dealing with Varied Rules and Disciplines

When divorced parents remarry, their children usually find themselves faced with one set of rules, or lack thereof, at the domicile home, and another set of rules, or lack thereof, in the other biological parent's home.

You may have heard statements like, "My dad lets me do that at his house," or "My mom lets me talk on the phone any time, and as late as I want." It is best if the two biological parents can minimize the differences in rules, but that is not always possible. After all, if the biological parents got along and agreed to work together, they would likely have never divorced.

The solution to this issue is not to relax or eliminate rules and discipline, for all children need boundaries and discipline. You should also not try to change the rules in the other home, which is impossible.

Instead, explain to your child the reasons for the rules you have established. If the rules pertain to moral issues, show your children God's reasons for the rules you have established.

Be patient with your children if they question or challenge the purpose of certain rules they must obey in your home, but not in the other home. Have sound reason, and be consistent.

Do not be intimidated by the two sets of rules that your children have in their two parents' homes. Consider that they also have different rules at Grandma's house, at football practice, in Mrs. Bella's algebra class, in Mr. Steve's economics class, and on the school bus. Your children know and adjust to different rules many times each day.

Understand that you cannot control your child or the rules when he or she is at their other parent's home. These are some of the times in your life when you have to release your children into the hands of your Almighty loving God. If you have great concern when they are with their other parent, pray for their protection. Then pray for them when they return to you (we will further discuss prayer in Chapter 9).

## Complex Lives

Children of divorce lead complicated lives, both logistically and emotionally. They are the ones who pack their bags and move from house to house for visitation, summer vacations, or holidays. (In rare instances do the parents move from house to house, allowing the children to stay in the same environment—and that usually ends when one biological parent remarries.)

In our Blended Family, Paige's girls lived with us and they visited their dad every other weekend. I had visitation two out of every three weekends until my son came to live with us the last two years of high school. The commute for Paige's girls was two hours round trip, and four hours round trip for my children.

We literally had to keep a calendar as to who was with us each weekend. If it was very difficult on us as parents, think of how difficult it was on our children to do this every month for years.

Some joint custody cases require the children to swap domicile residence every week. This arrangement is usually for the convenience of the parents, and some family counselors agree that it is not emotionally healthy for the children.

When going to school, children of divorce may frequently have to pack books and clothes because Dad is dropping them off and Mom will be picking them up to spend the next few nights with her.

We have asked some parents if they would like to pack their bags and live somewhere else every week, or every other weekend twelve months of every year. Most just stared at us and did not reply, but they got our message of the burden their children carry.

Some parents have tried to discount their children's peril with, "Children are resilient. They will be okay." Our reply to such thinking is, "How resilient are you? How long does it take you to bounce back from a major life change that continues to evolve?"

## They Miss Family and Friends

Someone is always missing. When children are with Mom, they miss Dad, and vice versa. They miss having Mom and Dad together

The experience is even worse for teenagers whose world revolves around their friends. While their friends from school are planning parties and get-togethers for the weekend or the summer, children of divorce may be leaving town to spend time with their other parent.

They are missing their mom, or their dad, or their friends, or school activities, or playing in a ball game.

While we agree that there is a strong need for children to spend time with both parents, they do not deserve this stressful lifestyle. Parents, please consider what you are subjecting your children to. Consider their feelings and how your decisions affect them. As a caring parent, please do your best to make life easier on your children. It is a tough balance to find, but their world needs to be balanced.

## The Blended Family Child's Family

When single parents remarry, their children's world changes more than we realize. Think about the size of the family that children in Blended Families interface with.

They can have up to two sets of parents/new parents, multiple siblings/new siblings/half-siblings, four sets of grandparents/new grandparents, and multiple aunts/new aunts, uncles/new uncles, and cousins/new cousins. When our children become adults and marry, they gain numerous in-laws and then begin a family of their own.

Their family life can become huge, complex, and difficult to manage. As the children marry and begin their own family, they may isolate themselves from the complexity.

As biological parents and new parents, we need to be understanding of our children's world. The fact is, we do not have to interact with all the people that are now in their lives.

We should embrace our children's world and the people within, to the best of our ability, making right choices when events bring people together.

We need to be the Christ-like example of love, kindness, acceptance, and serving.

We should be considerate of our children's schedules and their commitments to their other family members when we plan events and vacations where we want our children with us.

We need to be willing to sacrifice our wants and desires to accommodate the needs of our children.

These thoughts may not seem fair to you, but remember that your children did not ask for the divorce or death of a parent. Neither did they ask for the remarriage and blended family that they are now a part of. Through remarriage, we (their parents) have continued to add to their complex world. The least we can do is help them manage it and do our best to take any pressure off of them.

We call this "taking the high road" to help our children. The high road is not an easy road at first, because it requires us to give up things we want. But the more we give, the more we see these three things happen:

1. Our children see who is making life easier for them, and they truly appreciate it.
2. The more we receive from Father God and other people.
3. The more that giving becomes our lifestyle, and the more it becomes an easy, natural response for us.

## Action Steps

- Review your custody and visitation arrangements, and consider how you might make life better for your children.
- Consider how you and your child's other parent can work together better. Discuss any plans you make with your spouse.
- Look for opportunities to take the "high road" to accommodate all of your children (biological and new), making life easier for them.

## The Other Biological Parent

Children will always love their other biological parent—never expect them not to. If you have experienced divorce, you may still harbor some negative thoughts and ill feelings toward your former spouse. While you may not like the other biological parent, he or she will continue to be a vital part of your children's lives—whether in the physical realm or in their heart. More than likely, your children have already heard negative talk about, or have seen you exchange harsh words with, your former spouse.

We already discussed living a life of forgiveness in Chapter 2. Yet, as many times as you have prayed to forgive them and release them, ill feelings can creep in again. Realize that whoever angers you controls you.

Your former spouse may have caused great pain in your life. But if you are not walking in forgiveness, you are only hurting yourself and your children. Holding a grudge will choke the life out of you, your biological children, and your new family. You do not have to be best friends with a former spouse to act in kindness and to be polite and gracious.

During times when you are experiencing negative feelings, do not expect any of your children to feel the way you do, or to disrespect or not love their other biological parent. That parent is, and always will be, their parent, and will always have some influence on them.

Realize that God loves your former spouse and God requires you to forgive and to do good for him or her. We recommend that you avoid using the terms "ex-spouse" or "ex." These terms imply that the person is marked, and is a "has-been" who is no longer of value. He or she may not be of value to you, but God does not see the child's other parent that way. God always sees value, potential, and hope in everyone.

Admittedly, former spouses can be difficult. Some former spouses attempt to gain control over, or in other ways manipulate, their child's other family. If this is you and your former spouse has remarried, please let your former spouse move on. Your former spouse does not need you and should not allow you to run things. Give him or her some space, and your former spouse will likely give you some respect. Respect is always a two-way street. If you are not giving respect, you will likely not receive any. (The former spouse is further discussed in Chapter 7.)

## Action Steps

- Never ask your children about the other parent's life or lifestyle, unless there is sound reason to believe that there may be an illegal environment or abuse that affects the child. Keep questions to the child personal, such as, "What did you do this weekend? Did you have fun?" Then move on to other subjects.
- Do not discuss issues concerning the other parent in front of the children, unless it is of utmost importance to have the children's input. If your children make remarks about their other biological parent's behavior, lifestyle, or choice of discipline, do not comment. It is very important that the children only hear

you make positive comments about their parent.

- If tension exists, keep conversations between you and your former spouse short and non-emotional. Avoid confrontations. If confrontations do take place, spare your children from having to hear them.
- If you have unforgiveness toward your former spouse or your new spouse's former spouse, review and walk through the steps to forgiveness section in Chapter 2.

## Special Events

Like all children, children in Blended Families celebrate birthdays, graduations, weddings, and dozens of other special occasions. They may also participate in a variety of sports, dance classes, or other hobbies and activities.

It is important to your children to have both their biological parents and their new parents present (if bonding has been achieved) for these occasions. However, many children of divorce do not experience such parental support because the biological parents and former in-laws do not get along and may refuse to be in the same place with each other, or in the presence of their former spouse's new spouse.

In many cases, the children wind up having two separate birthday parties, or possibly having only one parent attend the ball game, the commencement ceremony, the dance review, the parent-teacher meeting, or even the wedding, all for the convenience of the parents who do not want to be around each other. In some situations, both biological parents attend major functions, but demonstrate ill will and cause friction; the child feels the tension and is made miserable. Some new spouses are excluded from the invite list of some or all of these events.

Two of our daughters got married within two years. Both weddings were marked by tension between former spouses and former in-laws. Frustrated and disgusted, one of our daughters asked me why her biological parents could not get along like adults for her wedding. It was a very good question, one to which I did not have a good answer.

As we mentioned earlier, children of divorce did not ask for their lifestyle. Children need their biological parents to be amicable and mature. Tension between former spouses must be eliminated for the welfare of your children.

Children should grow up in an atmosphere of love, mercy, and grace. It is the responsibility of all parents—biological and new—to create that atmosphere. Your children are worth it.

## Action Steps

- Put yourself in your child's place. Imagine what it would be like to have the people you love the most at odds with each other. Then make a commitment to improve the relationship between you and your former spouse.
- Do not speak in harsh tones, or be on the defensive.
- Change your attitude by looking for the good in your former spouse—there is good in everyone.
- Work to resolve the strained relationships between you and your former spouse (and former in-laws) so that all can attend your child's important events without creating tension. You may not be successful, but at least you have tried.
- Pursue true, complete forgiveness of your former spouse. Keep in mind that tolerance is not the same as true forgiveness (see Chapter 2).

- Communicate with your former spouse for the benefit of your children. When appropriate, attempt to have face-to-face meetings with your former spouse and new spouse to discuss your children's events, education, or other special needs. Always begin such meetings in prayer, asking that an attitude of cooperation and peace prevail. Never attempt such a meeting without prayer.

## The Pawn

Often a child of divorce is placed between his and her biological parents for the convenience of the parents. Some children are expected to deliver orders, messages, testify in court, and in other ways be the go-between. At times, an older child may become the parent's confidant, on which the parent unloads their feelings and burdens.

Your children do not want to be in the middle of two non-communicating, uncooperative adults. Your children did not ask for any of this. Stop using them.

To parents who use your children to bring division into your former spouse's new family—watch out for the bitter seeds that you sow. Your children are watching, and more than likely know that you are the troublemaker who is trying to stir up trouble in the other home. They feel your resentment and prying, and do not appreciate it. In your efforts to make life difficult for your former spouse, you are abusing your own children.

## Biological Parents and New Parents Helping Children

Oftentimes parents are not in touch with the magnitude of hurt within their children. We may realize they are hurting, but we likely do not understand the depth of the hurt. If the child is not open about their feelings, we may truly think that if we are okay they are okay. This is an unrealistic assumption.

Some children have a very difficult time coping with adversity, or with their negative feelings. They may not know how to let go of impossible dreams and will struggle for years.

As stated before, children will often talk to someone else before they will open up to their own parents because they do not want to risk angering, hurting, or alienating their parents. If you are not communicating with your children, or if they will not open up to you, consider other available help. Have them talk to a friend, pastor, children's church leader, youth group leader, or professional counselor.

## Action Steps

- We repeat the following statement because it is so important: Apologize to your children for the divorce. You likely did not intend to produce the hurt in your children. You may have done everything to try to reconcile the marriage. Yet, your apology may be the only one they will ever get.
- Commit to them that you will not put them through another divorce. This will reinforce to them that marriage is a covenant to be kept, and seeing you live your commitment will help break the cycle of divorce in their lives.
- Take a closer look at your children to identify their emotional state. Ask them how they are feeling. Show concern for their hurting hearts. Allow your children to vent and express themselves, while maintaining respect for each other. Do not react negatively when they are sharing their feelings, or they will not

open up to you again.

- Help them to set new realistic goals and dreams. Tell them the goals you have for your new family.
- If needed, seek professional counseling. A third party can often bring clarity and a new perspective.
- Pray for and with your children everyday.
- Stop pumping your children for information about your former spouse's life.
- Stop making it difficult for your former spouse to spend time with his or her children.
- Stop using your children. Take responsibility. Using children is immature.

If you are guilty of anything discussed in this chapter, resolve to end any negative attitudes or behavior *now*. Start by asking God your Father to forgive you. Then ask for your children's forgiveness. Then forgive yourself.

Focus on rebuilding your own life. We are so proud of people we know who are focused on improving themselves—going back to school, learning new trades, serving in areas of the church, or extending a helpful hand to those in need. They are moving on and into the new things God has for their lives, and so can you.

## Healthy Disclosure Needed

One of my daughters brought to my attention some things about our former family that had been kept from her. At the ages of seventeen and thirty-one, she heard some things from other family members about our former family, but some important facts were omitted.

The information disturbed her, and she was left to process the given information on her own.

Every family and every broken home has a story. Parents could be unaware of things that should be disclosed, or they may have intended to shield children from further hurt. But failure to disclose parts of a child's family information can actually cause more hurt and misunderstanding down the road. There may be things that are not easy to talk about with your child, but they need to be discussed.

Disclosing family information that has been withheld should always be done sooner rather than later, as soon as the child is old enough to understand. As a friend of mine says, "Delaying the delivery of unpleasant news never makes it good news."

We caution you to not use disclosure in an unhealthy way. Disclosure can be misused by an angry, hurt, or bitter parent in an attempt to discredit or devalue a child's other parent. Examples of unhealthy disclosure are:

- "Let me tell you what your father did to us."
- "Your mother cheated on me."
- "Your dad has not paid child support in the last two years."
- "Your mom is an alcoholic."
- "Your father is dead," when the truth is that he is living in another state or country.

There is no healing value for the child in any of the above statements.

The purpose of disclosing truth to your children is for their healing, not yours. Do not use this process to dump your burdens on your children. As stated earlier, children are not designed to be your support.

## When and What to Disclose

Young children cannot process complex or painful issues. Disclosure will be most effective when the child is a teen or older, and able to understand and properly process what you tell them.

As you prayerfully consider the things you need to disclose to a child, ask yourself these three questions:

1. "Is there anything about my life or my former marriage, past or present, that I have not told my child about because I do not want him or her to know?" If so, write them down.
2. "If my child finds out about personal family information (each item you wrote down in Question 1) from another source, will my child feel like I held information from him or her, and will my child have received the whole truth from that other source?"
3. "If I share that information, will it bring value and healing to my child?" If yes, then consider the right time and place to have a heart-to-heart.

## Adult Children

Divorce affects children of all ages and for years to come. Remarriage also affects children of all ages. Adult children continue to feel the effects of divorce as they develop families of their own. Grown children pick up the burden of planning birthday parties, perhaps for a grandchild, and special family events where family members of both biological parents are invited. In some cases they have to plan two parties to accommodate parents who refuse to be together.

As Nicole described earlier, this can become a stressful time for our grown children, in which they hope and pray that everyone will be at peace and enjoy their time at each event. We have experienced the tension that they dread at weddings.

Since such activities will continue for many years, it is all the more reason that parents need to walk in forgiveness and peace with everyone. Do your part as a mature Christian parent to make each event a positive, memorable event.

We mentioned in Chapter 3 that children of divorce long to see their parents reconcile. We have met adult children whose parents divorced many years ago and at least one parent has remarried. Some of these adult children have not been able to let that dream die and therefore fail to embrace their parents' new lives, new marriages, and new families.

Although adult children have grown up and, hopefully, have become successful, they still struggle with many of the nineteen "hesitant to connect" issues discussed earlier. Since they are now in control of their life, but might still be hurting, they will sometimes disconnect from one or both parents and their new families in the same way that you may have disconnected from a person who has hurt you. This behavior might include no calls or visits, not returning phone calls, refusal to attend the remarriage of a parent, denial of the remarriage, non-acceptance of a new parent, and not allowing grandparents to see their grandchildren.

This disconnect from family may be a temporary way for the adult child to deal with their negative emotions. They may need time alone to sort through their emotions. However, this behavior has also been used as emotional blackmail to hurt the ones who hurt them, or to attempt to change a parent. It can become a form of manipulation.

Many years ago I knew a widowed man who had four married sons. After a few years of living alone, he began to date someone, fell in love, and proposed marriage to her. The sons gave him a hard time about this new woman and refused to have anything to do with her. He loved his sons and this lady dearly and was so torn about what to do. It ended in suicide.

As we previously stated, hurting people hurt people. Negative behavior directed by adult children toward their divorced and/or remarried parents is driven by their hurting hearts. Their negative actions may be stating one or more of the many things we addressed with minor children.

Parents must not react to emotional blackmail from anyone. If we have a repentant heart, God has forgiven us. If we are allowing God to direct our steps, we should move into the new things that God is bringing forth in our life.

Although parents no longer have the direct influence over our adult children, they still influence their children's behavior (in a positive or negative way) through attitude, words, and actions. Pray for your children daily, asking God to heal their hurts and disappointments. Take the high road and continue to show acceptance of them, even if they do not accept you right now. Continue to extend God's grace and express unconditional love toward them.

## Action Steps

- Do not walk in guilt, or they will sense it and may continue to manipulate.
- Apologize to them for any hurts you may have caused.
- Regularly invite them to dinner and on vacations, even if you know or expect the answer to be "No." You are letting them know that they are a part of your family, and if they decline it is

their decision to not participate.

- Continue to call and leave messages letting them know that you love them and they are important to you and your new family.
- Do not react to their negative behavior by saying harsh words and attempting to make them feel guilty. This will only burn the bridge between you.

## Adult Children Living with You

If you have permitted an adult child to live with you, these adults may tend to want to live with no boundaries imposed on them. After all, they are adults, right?

We strongly recommend responsibilities and boundaries be established for everyone living in your home (including adult children) that are agreeable to you and your spouse, and which will maintain peace, order, and godliness. This is especially true if you still have minor children in your home who may be observing inappropriate behavior or subject matter from the adult child. It is necessary to protect the young hearts under your care, even if it requires standing up to the adult child's lifestyle.

## Our Prayer for You

Father, we ask You to help the parents in this Blended Family to be instruments of healing to their children. Show them the hearts of their children and what they are feeling, and help the parents be more understanding.

Forgive these parents for the times they may have been unfair to a child, reacted hastily, or used their children for their convenience. Help them to respect the feelings of each child. Help the parents walk in forgiveness toward the former spouses, and to build a healthy, loving, and caring environment in their home. Thank You for showing them Your loving hand in parenting.

If there are adult children, we pray for Your wisdom and breath to build unity and heal damaged relationships.

Father, breathe Your breath on this family—breathe on the children.

In Jesus compassion, and through the help of the Holy Spirit. Amen.

## Funny Family Moments

When our children were young they loved watching movies. Their favorites were *Flight of the Navigator*, *Mary Poppins*, *The Sound of Music*, and *Cinderella*. They had the lines of these movies memorized, so they would choose character roles, lie on the floor in front of the TV, start the movie and recite the movie lines while it was playing. It was quite entertaining!

Chapter 7

# Responsibilities of a New Parent

## *Paige Becnel*

*I don't really have the right words to express how it can be hard to plan events, get-togethers, celebrations, parties, weddings, graduations, baby dedications, christening, and such when there are multiple families (some that are divorced from each other) involved. It can just be hard . . . and complicated. People can get offended and opinionated.*

*And the stress always lies on the kids. It just does. And it shouldn't. You just want everyone to be happy and enjoy themselves for the sake of your child . . . or whoever the event is for. But sometimes everyone can't be happy . . . which unfortunately creates a lose-lose situation. Trying to be everyone to everybody and the peacemaker at the same time can be very exhausting and very overwhelming. I used to try to be all that, more than I do now, I think.*

*I remember certain aspects of wedding planning being very stressful for me . . . the dreaded seating arrangements, for example. Now, I have my own family and their needs come before anything. When we plan parties and occasions, I try to be considerate and accommodating, but I guess on some level I just hope that we have all forgiven and moved on and can let the past be the past, you know?*

*And I don't have the energy to worry too much about that anymore. Anyway . . . I know it can be hard. It can be hard to plan anything with groups of people who aren't friends on a day-to-day basis.* —Nicole

▪ ▪ ▪

BECOMING A GOOD NEW PARENT is one of the toughest assignments in the world. *Loving, caring for, and parenting a child who was not born to you is not a natural thing.* Attempting to cross into that arena is often out of your comfort zone.

But when you marry a man or woman with children, you have also married his or her children. A biological parent and child are intricately attached; you cannot separate them.

> *People were also bringing babies to Jesus to have Him touch them. When the disciples saw this, they rebuked them. But Jesus called the children to Him and said, "Let the little children come to Me, and do not hinder them, for the kingdom of God belongs to such as these. I tell you the truth, anyone who will not receive the kingdom of God like a little child will never enter it"*
> (Luke 18:15–17).

Jesus called children to Himself, touching each one of them. Why? Because He wanted to serve them, love them and bless them, just as He did and still does to you and me. God loves His cherished creation.

We are here to serve our children, to bless them, to love them, to nurture them, and to help them in every way possible. We are to lead them along the right paths in life.

This role may seem more, well, "natural" for the biological parent, but as you will see through this chapter, new parents are also charged with this responsibility. How can new parents do this? You begin in the following two ways.

## Be Yourself

In the movie *Stepmom*, Julia Roberts plays the stepmother-to-be to two children of divorce. In the beginning, Roberts' character exhausts her energies trying to become what and who the children's biological mother wants her to be. But only after she decides to stop imitating someone else and be herself do her new children begin to respect and love her.

Your new children want and need the real you, not some figment of your imagination. Show them who you really are. Don't try to impress them with wild antics, dress styles, or attitudes. Don't try to prove that you are "hip," or that you've "got it together."

Instead, simply show them that you are willing to do what it takes to make this family union work for them, their mother or father, and you. Laugh with them, cry with them, and talk to them about things going on in their lives.

They may not open up to you right away, but with time, love, patience, and the real you, they will come around. I can attest to this myself.

## Develop a "Spirit of Adoption"

I am not advocating that new parents should attempt to legally adopt their spouse's children unless the situation opens itself for that. In most cases the other biological parent would not allow you to legally adopt your spouse's children. I also do not suggest coercing the other biological parent into allowing a legal adoption, as the child would feel abandoned by that biological parent if this happened.

What I am suggesting instead is that you *mentally* and *emotionally* adopt. Consciously make your new children a vital part of your world.

The word *adopt* comes from the Latin word *adoptare*, which means "to choose." Webster's defines *adopt* as "to take by choice into a relationship." You made a choice to marry your spouse, along with his or her children. Now you must choose to blend together as a family. The children, no matter what their ages, are a vital part of your family.

While I was writing this section, Patrick and Ana, who are close friends of ours and a great Blended Family, experienced a trauma in their family. Patrick sent us this email:

> "On Friday Ana and I almost lost our son Adrian. He was in gym class playing basketball and he started gasping for breath and collapsed. His heart had stopped beating and he died. Thank God the school had a defibrillator (AED) in the gym and the coach, who was trained to use the AED, brought Adrian back to life. They air evacuated him to Children's Memorial Hermann Hospital in downtown Houston and he was in critical condition.
>
> "The name of his condition is much longer than I can pronounce, especially after not sleeping for more than forty-eight hours. But, short version is this. The septum (center wall) in his heart is unusually thicker than it should be and when he began playing ball, his heart started having an irregular beat causing him to go into cardiac arrest and sudden death. This is a genetic heart condition that was totally unknown to us. He has always been a very healthy, active boy.
>
> "But now his life will forever be changed, as ours will be

> too. They will implant an internal defibrillator in his chest to hopefully prevent this from ever happening again. This is not something you'd expect to hear about a sixteen-year-old boy, especially a healthy active boy.
>
> "I beg all of you for prayer for our son's life. He is the very beat of my heart, and I cannot imagine my life without my son. Needless to say, our lives have come to a complete stop and we are staying at his side 24/7. Please pray for my son." —Patrick

Read Patrick's last paragraph again. What is not obvious in this email is that Patrick never had biological children. He married Ana and married her three children. He *chose* her children as his own.

Moe and I called Patrick to check on Adrian's progress, and we discussed how (evident from the email) he has a deep heart connection to Adrian. He told us that he explained to the children more than once that anyone can birth children, and said to them, "But I have *chosen* you. This is even more significant than if I had birthed you."

Wow, what a profound statement! I immediately thought of the many children in biological homes who were "birthed," but became emotionally ignored, were put down, and developed behavioral problems because they never experienced true unconditional love and acceptance from their biological parents.

The Bible describes such a "spirit of adoption," through which you and I are made sons and daughters of God.

> *Because you are sons, God sent the Spirit of His Son into our hearts, the Spirit who calls out, "Abba, Father." So you are no longer a slave, but a son; and since you are a son, God has made you also an heir* (Galatians 4:6).

> *I will be a father to you, and you will be My sons and daughters, says the Lord Almighty* (2 Corinthians 6: 18).

> *But you are a chosen people, a royal priesthood, a holy nation, a people belonging to God, that you may declare the praises of Him who called you out of darkness into His wonderful light* (1 Peter 2: 9).

God chose us to be His own special people. *He chose you.* You are royal, holy, and you belong to God. He has called you into His light.

Those precious little ones who are now living with you, or who you have influence over, are waiting for you to call them into your light, your world, your love. Make a choice to choose them.

If you do not have this spirit of adoption toward your new children, ask God to help you find it. Just the conscious act of asking God will begin to unify your family in an incredible way.

It took our family a while to understand the concept and realize the benefits of the spirit of adoption discussed above. But as Moe and I committed to choose our new children as our own, our love grew and we worked to treat all of our children equally. Acceptance of each other and appreciation for each other grew and reached new levels.

To commemorate our early wedding anniversaries, Moe not only brought me a card and a gift, but also brought our children cards and presents. The occasion became not just Paige and Moe's wedding anniversary, but an anniversary of our Blended Family—an anniversary of our new children's lives with us.

> *Sons are a heritage from the Lord, children a reward from Him* (Psalm 127: 3).

All children are a blessing. God sees no bloodlines (other than the blood of Jesus that redeemed us back to Him), and neither should you. Remember, Jesus called the little children to Himself, and rebuked the disciples for trying to send them away.

Are you calling the children in your house to you, or are you pushing them away? If you have been pushing them away, don't let guilt overcome you. Make a choice to right the wrong. Children are very forgiving, and so is God. Begin today to surround yourself with your children. Call your new children your sons and daughters. Make them your heirs. You can help fill the void in their hearts left by death or divorce. You can be the tool God uses to heal their broken hearts. God is doing the very same thing for you.

## Legal Aspects

We are well aware that, as new moms and new dads, we have no legal rights over the new children in our lives, unless we were able to legally adopt them. And we are not trying to circumvent that authority in anything we say in this book. As an example, we cannot legally take them to a doctor or pick them up from school without a biological parent's permission. In Blended Families the biological parents have legal guardianship over their children. However, we believe a new parent's concern for his or her new children needs to be at the same level as the children's biological parents.

To avoid any legal issues with a biological parent, do not attempt to make any decisions about your new child. Allow the biological parent to make the decisions.

As new parents we need to always respect the legal authority of the biological parents. At the same time, the biological parents need to respect each other's spouses and realize that decisions concerning the children should be done with input from all the spouses since the decisions made about the children will ultimately affect everyone involved.

## God's Gift of Favor

As new parents we often make a concerted effort to draw close to our new children, but we can become frustrated. Some children may not be ready for the new relationship for one or more of the nineteen reasons previously discussed in Chapter 5. Perhaps our lack of caring, lack of attention, lack of patience, harsh words, or inappropriate actions is pushing the children away from us. Building a new relationship takes time, but we are always impatient.

If you have already made consistent positive efforts to develop relationships and have become frustrated, God can help you. There are many references in the Bible where God grants people favor with Him, and with men. The story of Joseph in Genesis Chapters 37 to 41 shows God's favor on the life of a man who goes from being cast out of his family and thrown into prison to becoming the Prime Minister of Egypt.

> *For surely, O LORD, you bless the righteous; you surround them with your favor as with a shield* (Job 10:12).

> *Let love and faithfulness never leave you; bind them around your neck, write them on the tablet of your heart. Then you will win favor and a good name in the sight of God and man* (Proverbs 3:3–4).

When our acts of loving include faithfulness (not complacency or inconsistency), God can give us favor with the new children in our life. Since divine favor is from God, ask God for favor with your new children.

## Vows to Your New Children—It's Never Too Late

One of the greatest tools you can use to connect to your children, and help them to connect to your new Blended Family, is for each new parent to make vows to each new child.

Too often, spouses underestimate just how large of a part the new children will play in the new marriage, regardless of the children's age. When children do not feel a part of the new marriage and family, or when a child is resistant to the new spouse or family, great turmoil and stress often develops in the weeks, months and years ahead.

We continue to stress this important reality: Your spouse and their biological children were and are "one" before you and your spouse vowed to become "one" in marriage. *Your marriage vows with your spouse do not circumvent the relationship they have with their children.* Many spouses have tried to separate their spouse from their biological children by making their spouse choose between them and their biological children, or by causing a child or children to feel unwelcome in the home.

Here is a solution: Instead of making your spouse have to periodically make an unfair choice between you and their children, *you make the choice to be in covenant with their children*. It is time to stop being a "step"-parent. Choose to love them. Choose to make them an integral part of your life. Just as you made vows to your spouse, make vows to your spouse's children.

## The Benefits of Children's Vows

When you share vows with children you will accomplish the four following things for your marriage and family:

1. You will make the children feel significant—that they are a real part of your life and the new home and not just on the sideline. It is so important to get all members of your family started off in the right mindset. The sooner you create the right atmosphere and attitudes, the better.
2. The attention that you give them during the vows will let them know that they are important to you, and to the new family.
3. You will become more aware of their presence in your home, and of your responsibility toward them.
4. You will enhance the relationship between you and your spouse. When you embrace your spouse's children, you embrace your spouse more completely.

## Already Married? Do It Anyway!

Maybe you and your spouse chose the out-of-town island wedding. Perhaps your children were too young when you married, or maybe you just did not think of including your children to this extent in your wedding. That's okay. The good news is that it's not too late. It is never too late to develop deeper relationships and to let people know you accept them into your life. (See Appendix C for sample children's vows.)

## Action Steps

- Choose to make your new children a vital part of your world.
- During the first year of marriage, build caring relationships with your new children.

- Do not discipline your new children during the first year of marriage; allow their biological parent to do so. Love must cover discipline.
- Remember, what's good for your biological child is good for your new child, too. Make all of the rules the same for everyone. If you bring home surprise gifts, include everyone.
- Give every child a chance to express his or her thoughts at family meetings.
- Eliminate favoritism. Do not treat any child like a Cinderella or Prince Charming.
- Arrange schedules so that everyone goes on vacation together as one family.
- Spend money equally on each child at Christmas, on birthdays, and throughout the year.
- Ask God for His hand of favor over your life.
- Share vows with your new children. If you are already married, prepare a special occasion to share vows (see Appendix C).

## Our Prayer for New Parents

God, we pray for the new parents in this Blended Family. Help them to continually walk in grace toward their new family. Remind them daily that You created them to be exactly who they are and not someone else. Thank You for choosing us and loving us as sons and daughters. Help the new parent to choose the new children You have brought into their family. Strengthen each parent to make the right decisions every day based on Your love, mercy, grace, and principles. We thank You that Your Holy Spirit is in them and guiding them. In Jesus our Savior's name. Amen.

## Responsibilities of a New Father

Moe asked me to write this section, not because I am a father, but because I could see what my children needed in a new fatherly role model in our home.

If you have biological children, you may be thinking, "I'm already a father. What's the difference between parenting and parenting a new child?" For answers, let's look at Jesus' family life with Mary and Joseph.

Most of us know the story of the Immaculate Conception of Jesus. In Matthew 1:18–24, Joseph and Mary were engaged to be married when Mary, through the Holy Spirit, became pregnant with God's Son. God sent an angel to Mary to reveal to her the details of His plan, and to explain the remarkable circumstances surrounding her pregnancy.

Now imagine Joseph's reaction upon hearing this news. His fiancé was pregnant, and the baby was not his. And no matter how much he cared for and respected Mary, could Joseph really believe her explanation for the pregnancy?

While we will never know all of Joseph's thoughts, one thing is certain. Joseph truly did love Mary—enough to save her life. Jewish law dictated that a woman found pregnant out of wedlock was to be stoned to death. Instead, Joseph made plans to send Mary away quietly to have her child.

During this time Joseph experienced a lot of confusion, just as many new parents do. What do I do? What is my responsibility? Help me Lord!

But then, an angel visited Joseph and confirmed to him that Mary's child was of the Holy Spirit. And wonder of wonders, God had chosen him, a simple carpenter, to care for and parent the Son of God!

> *But after he had considered this, an angel of the Lord appeared to him in a dream and said, "Joseph son of David, do not be afraid to take Mary home as your wife, because what is conceived in her is from the Holy Spirit. She will give birth to a Son, and you are to give Him the name Jesus because He will save His people from their sins* (Matthew 1:20–21).

Joseph was to marry Mary and he, Joseph, was to name the child Jesus. Naming children was the role of fathers in Israelite custom. By giving the directive to Joseph to name the child, the angel of the Lord was giving Joseph the responsibilities and influence of fatherhood for the child Jesus. Wow! Joseph was to provide a good home in which to raise their son. *Their* son—now that is a thought. How could the Son of God be their son? Because Joseph was to be Mary's husband. When he married Mary, he also married her unborn child.

Can you imagine being called to become the new father of the Son of God? What a challenge Joseph faced! How did he handle it? He provided the same love, discipline, and care for this child that he would later provide for his own biological children.

You may be thinking, "But Jesus was God's Son!" *So is the child you are now a new parent to.* Is not God the creator of all things and all people? When you accept Christ as your savior, you are a child of God. The same is true for any new children who have become part of your new family. Your new children may not yet have accepted Jesus as their Lord, but they need the same love, discipline, and care that you give to your very own child.

Perhaps you are now thinking, "I am not their father; they already have a father." So did Jesus. But this did not excuse Joseph from his responsibilities. It is not an excuse for you, either. In fact, the Scripture provides us with clear insight into the Blended Family of Joseph, Mary, and Jesus.

> *Now Jesus Himself was about thirty years old when He began His ministry. He was the son, so it was thought, of Joseph* (Luke 3:23).

Those around Mary and Joseph did not even know that Jesus was not Joseph's biological son.

I can imagine this family—Mary, Joseph, Jesus, as well as Mary and Joseph's other children (see Mark 3:32)—making their way through the town of Nazareth. I can see Mary and Joseph talking with neighbors while their children played together, maybe engaging in a game of chase or hide and seek among the merchants and their wares. I can picture Mary and Joseph keeping a careful eye on each child, including Jesus. I can imagine Mary and Joseph correcting them, carrying them, running after them, and laughing with them. Joseph's dedication and actions led people to never suspect that Jesus was not Joseph's biological son.

Luke Chapter 2 provides another look at Joseph's relationship with Jesus. Every year, Joseph took his family to Jerusalem for the Feast of the Passover. One year, a full day into their journey back home, Mary and Joseph noticed that twelve-year-old Jesus was not with them.

The Bible does not say that Mary went alone to look for her son. Instead, the Scripture tells us that both Mary and Joseph went back together to look for Jesus. They were both frightened, I am sure, and looked diligently for their son for three days before eventually finding Him in the temple courts (see Luke 2:41–47).

This account tells us that Mary and Joseph's marriage was not a "he is your son" arrangement. This was *their* family, and Joseph held himself responsible for the well being of Jesus.

Joseph loved Jesus as his son, his firstborn son, his and Mary's son. This does not mean that Joseph did not honor God as Jesus' Father, but that while Jesus was in his care, Joseph would treat Him as his own.

## The New Father Role

Just as Joseph was responsible for Jesus, you are responsible for the well being of each member of your new family when they are in your care. *You are not taking the place of your new children's birth father (although some of you may actually be acting in that role), but you have just as much influence over them.*

You may or may not see your new children every day, but what you say, how you discipline, how you behave, and your relationship with each new child is vital. The idea of "mine" and "yours" should not affect the way you care for and protect your new family. You are responsible for them.

Fathers provide the following three things for their children:

1. Provision—spiritual and financial. A father guides the children to know and accept Father God as their savior and Lord, and to develop and grow a personal relationship with God. A father also provides financial needs and blessings equally to all the children in the home.
2. Identity—A father can make every child feel that they belong, and are important and significant. The name conflict described earlier can be overcome in your home. (The Becnel home needed to become the Becnel-Morriz home.)

3. Security—A father who provides a safe, peaceful, stable, and loving home will produce courage in the children.

Some children may have a hard time accepting a new father figure. If this has happened to you, please understand that they did not choose you; you chose their mother and she chose you. The children may feel as though you have taken their mother's attention away from them; in a way, you have. But if you give them enough understanding, love, and patience, you will find that they will heal from this hurt and adjust.

The best way to handle such situations is for the biological parent to spend time with each biological child, one on one. You need to do the same with your biological children, one at a time. This time leads to the creation of special moments between each child and their parent. Everyone needs to feel special, needed, and accepted.

In our home, I took my daughters to lunch, to the movies, or to get a snow cone—just us. But I spent time with our other children as well. When we did things together as a family, my daughters were expected to participate.

> *It [love] always protects, always trusts, always hopes, always perseveres. Love never fails* (1 Corinthians 13: 7–8).

In another example of his close relationship with Jesus, the Bible tells us that Joseph taught his new son the family business—carpentry (see Mark 6:3). Together, they learned to build things out of pieces of wood, and to repair those things that were broken.

God our Father is also in the carpentry business. He makes wonderful things out of our pieces, and fixes what is broken in our lives. A Blended Family can be a wonderful restoration of what was broken.

## Our Prayer for the New Father

Father God, we pray that the new dad reading this begins to understand how important and special each member of his family is. We thank You that You hand-picked each person to be a vital part of this family. Teach this new father the same grace, patience, and love for others that was so evident in the life of Joseph. Fix what is broken in their lives, and build something using what seem to be fragments from the past. We love You Jesus and thank You for all that You are doing in us. Amen.

## The Role of a New Mother

Mention the word "stepmother" and the first thought that comes to mind is "wicked." The evil fairy tale stepmothers battled by Cinderella and Snow White seem to have become the standard image people have of a stepmother.

In the movie *Stepmom*, the Julia Roberts character struggles against this image. No matter how hard she tries, nothing she does is ever good enough, especially when her efforts are compared to those of the children's biological mother. Every encounter with her new children leaves her feeling like a failure—a flop who will never measure up.

As a new "new mother," I often felt the same way, struggling to define my role as a new mother when my new children were in my care. Then I realized a simple truth. The role of a *new* mother is the same as the role of *any* mother. Make a list of what you do or would do as a mother. You would love, nurture, train, teach, discipline, care for, encourage, and nurse. You would join carpools, make school lunches, chaperone field trips, teach to drive, shop for prom dresses, and babysit grandchildren.

You would partake in every aspect of your children's lives. And as much as possible, you should partake in your new children's lives.

When Moe and I were first married, I had a difficult time being a good mother to both my biological children and my new children. After all, my new children already had a mother. I was not interested in taking on her role, too. Eventually, I realized that I was not replacing her, but that I had been given the chance to nurture and help raise a part of Moe.

God made the wife and mother the very backbone of a home. When my children are not feeling well, I am the one they want. When Moe comes home from the office, I am the one he wants to talk to. If something cannot be found around the house, they usually come calling for me. On any given day, I hear . . .

- "Mom, have you seen my school shirt?"
- "Mom, did you put fruit in my lunch?"
- "Mom, did you wash my shorts yet?"
- "Mom, can you pick me up from work today?"
- "Mom, Mom, Mom, Mom!"

I hear these questions from *all* of our children (and from Moe, too). And I would gladly wash for, drive for, pack a lunch for, iron a shirt for, or do virtually anything for all of the children under my care, new or biological.

A mother provides the following three things for her children:

1. A "nesting instinct" that turns a house into a home. I love entering a "warm" home because you can sense a peace there. The nesting instinct creates that peaceful environment, and your whole family needs that peace.
2. Intuition—a sense about things that serves as a warning for the

family. When our children would bring a new friend over, they knew that I would get either a "good" or "bad" feeling about their friend. They would cringe in anticipation of the awaited verdict whether I sensed the friend was good for them to hang around. (We all become the company we keep, so we protected our children from bad company. Children do not have the ability to judge character, so they can get involved with the wrong people quickly.)

3. Spiritual sensitivity—women generally tend to be more spiritually connected than men, (though not in all cases). They tend to give more attention to reverence of God and their prayer time. The Holy Spirit has used that gift in women to get their families through many tough times.

Some children may have a hard time accepting a new mother figure. Again, you must understand that they did not choose you; you chose their father and he chose you. The children may feel as though you have taken their father's attention away from them; in a way, you have. But if you give them enough understanding, love, and patience, you will find that they will heal from this hurt and adjust.

We stated earlier that you may have more patience with your own children than your spouse's children. I was often guilty of imposing stricter rules on my new children than I would have on my own. I overcame this by asking myself each time if the rule or discipline I was imposing was the same rule I would ask my biological children to follow.

Ask yourself, "How would I handle this situation if this were my biological child?"

Your role as a new mother is no different than your role as a biological mother. Working as a team with your husband, you are to train the children you have been blessed to help raise with the same love, care, and devotion you would your biological children. How do you do this? With lots of love, understanding, kindness and patience. If you are filling a parent role to new children when they are with you, the same attitude of love, understanding, kindness and patience is required. Otherwise, you will become the "wicked stepmother."

## Our Prayer for the New Mother

Father God, we pray for this mother who longs to feel Your love for this new child in her life. Give her an understanding of who she has been given the privilege to help raise. Help her to make sound decisions on behalf of the welfare of this little lamb. Give her the grace to go on when she feels overwhelmed, and the joy that only You can give when her days seem to never end. Extend Your patience when hers has been spent. Pour out Your blessing into her heart. We love You so much, we thank You for always staying by our side. In Jesus name. Amen.

## Your Legacy in God's Eyes

Have you seen the movie *It's A Wonderful Life* with Jimmy Stewart and Donna Reed? It comes on television every Christmas season. It is a wonderful story about a man named George Bailey who owns a bank and building company in Bedford Falls. A character in town named Mr. Potter, who is a shrewd competitor, tries in many ways to put George out of business so he can buy the Bailey Savings & Loan Company and run the whole town.

Hard times fall on George and his family, and he wishes he had never been born. Clarence, George's guardian angel, shows up and takes George on a journey of what the world would look like if he had never been born.

It was quite eye-opening how the events of George's life and his interaction with people around him—from childhood to adulthood—affected everyone, and an entire community, with him and without him.

Everyone is an influencer. Think about all of the people in your life who have had an influence on you. You have great memories of some people, and bad memories of others. You are who you are in large part because of the influence of others, and from opportunities you were given or denied.

Consider the life you are building. Your life has a ripple effect. Your words, actions, and interactions with people around you—from childhood to adulthood—affect many people in your family, and your entire community, either in a good way as George Bailey did, or in a negative way as Mr. Potter did.

The impact you make on each person will ripple through their life to others they influence, and so on.

Consider the fact that Joseph's legacy (what we read about his life in the Holy Bible) is based on his relationship to Jesus the Son of God. Joseph's legacy is not based on his involvement with his biological children. Joseph is listed in the lineage of Jesus, even though they were not biologically related (see Matthew 1:16).

My point is this: You never know who God has placed in your home, under your care, or in your sphere of influence. It is vital that you sense your destiny toward those who God has brought into your world.

In tough times, we tend to question God and His understanding of where we are and of the people in our lives. God placed Jesus His Son in the hands of an earthly father figure whom He had personally hand picked. In the same way, God has personally hand picked you to be a motherly or fatherly role model; and a godly example to children who are not your own.

> *The righteous man leads a blameless life; blessed are his children after him* (Proverbs 20:7).

We have a great opportunity to leave our children a great legacy, one in which building a strong healthy family is of utmost importance, and divorce is not an option. All problems in a family can be solved; the solutions come when we start serving each other and stop being selfish. Solutions to our problems are discovered in God's Word and in our prayer time with God. He will show us how to respond (not react) to every situation. You see, God hates divorce, and He is deeply interested in seeing your marriage last a lifetime.

We must be intentional in developing a legacy worth having. It does not just happen.

## Action Steps

- Love your biological and new children with your actions—give them your time, encourage them, listen to them, extend forgiveness, and extend grace.
- Pray for your biological and new children everyday—for protection, health, acceptance, favor with others, for the friends they choose, and for their future. The Becnels prayed for our children's future spouses, and God answered those prayers beyond what we could have hoped for or imagined.
- Teach your biological and new children to love others—regularly visit a nursing home or a friend in the hospital or help someone move or prepare a meal for a family who is experiencing trauma,

and bring your children with you.

- Help your biological and new children to find God's plan for their life. Take them to church. Establish a high moral standard in your home, with high expectations. Teach them how to pray and how to forgive.

We pray that everyone who reads this will get a revelation that they control the legacy they leave. Each day you plant seeds in life that become your harvest. Be sure to plant good seeds, and not weeds, so that your life might be full.

Will you take the challenge that Joseph took? Will you be there when your new children need you, and even when they think they don't? Will you teach them the family business of restoration? Will you encourage them and guide them through life?

We pray that you will.

## Our Prayer for You

Father we ask you to bless the hands of the biological and new parents in this home. Give them Your heart of love and compassion for every family member. Give them the mind of Christ and guide their steps each day. Strengthen them when they become frustrated and exhausted.

Show them a glimpse of the awesome family they can become. Day by day, help each spouse to make right choices and build a legacy that will prosper their children and grandchildren. We pray in Jesus' mighty name. Amen.

## Funny Family Moments

One day Nicole and Kristen were pretending to put on a cooking show for Mom. They were being really goofy; it was just one of those days they couldn't stop giggling. Kristen was being really dramatic and acting like she was a chef. She was even using an accent she made up. The really funny part was when Nicole measured the vanilla and handed it to Kristen and jokingly told her to taste it. Nicole didn't realize that Kristen didn't know vanilla doesn't taste like it smells. So in her full dramatic chef character, Kristen took a big sip of the vanilla. Her eyes got huge and we all busted out laughing!

Chapter 8

# Interference From Extended Family

*Moe Becnel*

*One day a few years ago I was telling a man I had just met about Blending A Family Ministry. He said, "Oh, I am getting ready to be a Blended Family. I am marrying a beautiful lady who has never been married" He continued, "I am concerned for my ten-year-old daughter because my future father-in-law told me I would be his son-in-law, but my daughter would not be his granddaughter."* —Paige

▪ ▪ ▪

*For this reason a man will leave his father and mother and be united to his wife, and they will become one flesh* (Genesis 2:24).

IN OUR DISCUSSION of this verse in Chapter 2, we identified a potentially negative influence in a marriage—parents and extended family. God is giving us a warning about extended families and the negative effect they can have in marriage relationships. As we stated earlier, we personally know of marriages that have failed due to parental interference. Add the special pressures unique to a Blended Family, and the situation becomes even more unstable.

Many Blended Families suffer from some extended family members (parents, brothers, sisters, aunts, uncles, close friends, former spouses, etc.) who initially do not accept a new spouse or new children into their world. Such people may still be hurting from effects of the previous divorce. Some people seem to have a limit as to how much love they have to give, or they seem unable to love across the bloodline.

We know Blended Families in which extended family members do not like, and refuse to associate with, a new spouse or new children in the Blended Family. We have also seen extended family members give Christmas and birthday gifts to their biological grandchildren, nieces, and nephews, but ignore the new children in the same family.

The new spouse and new children naturally feel rejected and hurt. Under these situations, the new family environment becomes a place of hurt and separation rather than a place of healing and acceptance.

Cedric and Laura, whose marriage created a Blended Family, shared their story with us. Laura's extended family treated Cedric's children differently than they did Laura's biological children. Laura's parents did refer to Cedric's children as their grandchildren, but their actions they kept Cedric and his children at arm's length.

One day Laura's parents asked Laura for permission to take the grandchildren to Disney World in Orlando. However, their offer did not include Cedric's children. Needless to say, this hurt Cedric's children, it hurt Cedric, and it hurt Laura. Without words, a declaration had been made that Cedric's children (Laura's new children) were not accepted as family members by Laura's extended family.

Laura talked to her father about the hurt feelings, and out of guilt her father later invited Cedric's children on the vacation. Hurt feelings solved? Not quite.

Over the next several months, Laura noticed that her parents and siblings were not friendly toward Cedric and his children. Laura finally asked her extended family why they were cold toward her new husband and children. Of course, one of her siblings cited the vacation extended to Cedric's children. It was apparent that there was discontentment within Laura's extended family (parents and four siblings) because her parents had taken Cedric's children on vacation.

Cedric and Laura did not intend to cause problems between Laura and her parents and siblings. The issue was not Disney World. The real issue was acceptance. Laura merely wanted her extended family to accept her new husband and new children. Instead, she learned the age-old truth that you cannot make people love one another.

Some of you may agree with Laura's extended family. You may feel the new children were not really a part of the extended family, and may empathize with Laura's parents for wanting to have a vacation with their "real" grandchildren. If so, I ask you these questions:

- Would you feel differently if Cedric and Laura had adopted children together? If so, why?
- Why can't some people be accepting of others into their family or into their world?
- What does Jesus say about such a situation?

> *If you love those who love you, what credit is that to you? Even sinners love those who love them. And if you do good to those who are good to you, what credit is that to you? Even sinners do that. And if you lend to those from whom you expect repayment, what credit is that to you? Even sinners lend to sinners, expecting to be repaid in full. But love your enemies, do good to them, and lend to*

> *them without expecting to get anything back. Then your reward will be great, and you will be sons of the Most High, because he is kind to the ungrateful and wicked* (Luke 6: 32–35).

We certainly do not classify Cedric and his children as "enemies" to Laura's extended family. Yet, there was little intent by Laura's extended family to embrace her new family. If we cannot love beyond the boundaries of "blood (biological) family," we are not walking in the love that God requires.

There is an old saying, "Blood is thicker than water." Our culture today has understood the meaning of this phrase to be that biological (blood) family relationships are supposed to be stronger than all other relationships.

Yet, Jesus spoke of the New Covenant He came to make with mankind through the shedding of His blood.

> *In the same way, after the supper He took the cup, saying, "This cup is the new covenant in My blood, which is poured out for you"* (Luke 22:20).

When we accept Christ as our Savior and Lord, we are accepting His blood covenant over and above all other relationships in our life. Recall in Ephesians 5:25 where the Bible instructs husbands to love their wives just as Christ loves the Church and gave Himself up for her. In essence, we are to live in a blood covenant with our spouses, not with our biological family.

And as we discussed earlier, God tells us in Genesis 2:24 to leave our blood family and cling to our spouse through the marriage covenant we made.

Today I give you this new saying, based on God's Word in Genesis 2:24: *Marriage and family must be thicker than your biological family.* I consider my relationship with Paige, to whom I am joined in covenant before God, to be of more value than all other relationships in my life.

Laura's husband and new children were not "water" to her. Cedric was her new spouse that she made a covenant with. Her new family had been given to her by God, sealed by the covenant of marriage, and she cherished them all.

When Laura realized that her extended family did not accept her new family, she had three choices:

1. Ally with her extended family.
2. Ally with her new family.
3. Do nothing, which was already creating negative consequences within her new family.

The decision was not difficult to make, but it was difficult to carry out because she loved both families. Based on Genesis 2:24, Laura chose to stand by her new family and to stand up to her extended family. As long as her extended family refused to embrace her new family, there would be no true relationship with Laura. In other words, if Laura's extended family could not love her new family, they did not love her fully because she and her new family were one.

If Laura had decided to continue a "side" relationship with her extended family to ally with them —going to see them without her husband and new children—she would not have been living in covenant with her husband. And if she had decided to do nothing, ignoring the situation and hoping it would go away, she would not have been standing up for her new family.

Why do we tell this story of Cedric and Laura? Because many Blended Families have had similar experiences, often with disastrous, painful results. When a spouse abides by and makes decisions based upon the actions, opinions, desires, or advice of his or her parents and extended family rather than the opinions, desires, or advice of his or her spouse, he or she is not living in covenant as God intended.

## Honoring Versus Obeying

You may be thinking of another scripture, one of the Ten Commandments, which seems to contradict the above advice.

> *Honor your father and your mother, so that you may live long in the land the Lord your God is giving you* (Exodus 20:12).

I completely agree with this verse, but some may misunderstand it. Some grown children think honoring their parents means they must continue to listen to them, take their advice, or in other ways obey them. There may be misunderstanding in the meanings of the two words, "honor" and "obey."

Webster's defines *honor* as "esteem paid to worth, dignity, exalted rank or place, reverence; any mark of respect or estimation by words or actions." As an example, Paige and I honor our parents every time we make time to go visit them, send them a card, call to check on them, and help them with repairs at their homes. I honored my dad when he became ill by cutting his grass every week during the summer months.

*Obey* is defined as "to give an ear, to comply with the commands of, to be under the government of, to be ruled by, to submit to the direction or control of, to submit to commands or authority."

The best professional baseball and football players are "honored" when they are inducted into their respective halls of fame. This does not mean we now need to obey them. We can honor someone without letting him or her control our lives. Married children are to continue to honor extended parents and family. Yet, we are also to honor our spouses, and the highest place of honor must go to one's spouse.

## Parents Who Control

Many parents initially resist the process of their children "leaving father and mother" when their children marry. They may struggle to let go of the protectiveness or control they have had over their children for so many years. These extended parents sometimes revert to manipulation and guilt, making their married children feel guilty because they do not visit often enough, call every week, consult them about decisions in the new couple's marriage, or otherwise do as the parents directed them to.

Extended parents may offer large financial gifts or loans in an effort to exert persuasion or control over the couple. (Not every financial gift has strings attached, but many do.) Controlling parents may also presume that their child's spouse is the cause for their inability to control their married child. Most spouses who marry into a controlling extended family hope that their new spouse matures and breaks the apron strings. They intended to marry the individual, not an extended family network. Consider the TV sitcom *Raymond*, where the mother is regularly interfering in Raymond's marriage and family business. Although the TV sitcom goes to the extreme to create humor, there really are parent/grown child relationships similar to that.

Some new spouses have received blame from their new in-laws.

"You are the reason Bill does not come visit us every weekend."

"You have brought division in our family—our former daughter-in-law allowed us to keep our grandchildren until Steve married you."

Such blame will create unfounded guilt in your new spouse, a strained marriage relationship, as well as poor relationships between the in-laws.

Extended parents must learn to let their grown children lead their own lives. No good extended parent wants their children to make the same mistakes they did, but parents should only offer advice to grown children when it is asked for, then let the issue go. The best service a parent of married children can provide is to be there to help—but only when they are asked to help.

If you have controlling parents, you must take control of your life for the sake of your marriage. God's command to leave your father and mother and be united with your spouse means that your spouse now takes precedence over your parents and all other extended family.

## Standing Up for Your New Family

The situation becomes even more complicated when new children are involved. We do not know why some people can love anyone and love easily, even to the extent of being foster parents or adopting children, yet others cannot accept people outside of their "blood" family. We will not attempt to address the causes, other than to again say that hurting people hurt other people.

We must emphasize, however, that such behavior by your extended family has great potential to cause problems in your new family. Spouses in a Blended Family must stand up for every member of their new family. You have the responsibility to guard your new family against hurt.

If Laura had not stood up for her new husband and children, then she would have become another instrument of hurt to them. Likewise, if you do not protect your new family from hurts by your extended family, you become another instrument of hurt to them. You show them that you do not value them any more than your extended family does. The result is additional division and resentment in your home.

Look for signs of any hurtful words or actions from your extended family toward your new family. A good test is during the holidays—are all the children in your home treated equally by your extended family? It is important to identify who is not embracing your family. You can then discuss your new family with them.

We know it is very difficult to stand up to your extended family. But when they are hurting people who have done nothing to them, to do and to say nothing to them is negligence on your part. Tough situations require tough, yet gentle, actions.

Finally, keep in mind that while you cannot change people, God can. Pray over such situations. Ask God to change the hearts of the extended family members. Then be patient, and continue to protect the tender hearts of your new spouse and new children.

Extended family is important. The goal of this chapter is to identify and stop hurtful words and behavior, and to grow your family and extended family relationships. God wants to bring healing and complete restoration to your marriage, and to the extended family relationships. Your ultimate goal is that your extended family would love, embrace and be a part of your new family, and that your new family would love, embrace and accept them also.

Walk in love toward everyone, even those trying to bring division in your life.

## Reaching Out

What can you do to reach out to a difficult extended family member? As an example, let's say your sister does not like your new husband and avoids him at family functions. Here are some ideas to consider:

- Invite her to dinner so she can get to know your husband. (People often pre-judge others before they allow a chance to get to know them.)
- Offer to baby-sit her children one night.
- Be there for your sister during a time of need.
- Ask God for a creative idea to serve your sister

## Difficult Former Spouses

There are former spouses who continue to respect each other and work together for the greater good of the children involved. Some continue to be friends and get together as couples, although these situations are rare. We realize each case is different and so the level of difficulty to manage the new home and the children's affairs varies widely.

In this chapter of discussing interference from others, we want to give attention and understanding to difficult former spouses who may be creating interference and strife in your new home. Consider these questions:

- Have you had issues with one or both former spouses?
- Does a former spouse try to control or in other ways make troubled waters in your family?
- Do you have hard feelings toward your former spouse, or your spouse's former spouse?
- Does the troublesome former spouse have legitimate reasons for having hard feelings toward one of you?

- Are you a difficult former spouse, generating strife in another home?

We have heard from many families who call or write us about various issues that they have with a former spouse. It is a common problem. Let's look at common causes of the strife, and some reasonable solutions you might want to consider.

## Understanding the Strife

We previously discussed the fact that each of us needs to become individually whole and unload our hurts and past baggage. We also addressed how our children are also hurt from death of a parent or through divorce, and how as long as they are hurting they will bring hurt into other people's lives.

Likewise, former spouses may be stirring up trouble in your family because they are carrying hurts or past baggage. There could be other reasons as described below:

1. a.) Your former spouse may still be hurting from the breakup of your marriage. Rejection from a former love is a deep hurt that can take a long time to heal, especially if there was infidelity (adultery), rejection, or abuse involved in the prior marriage. If they are still hurting, prolonged hurt can lead to unforgiveness, bitterness, and ultimately revenge.

   b.) Right or wrong, your former spouse may sense (or know) that you left them for your new spouse, which makes them bitter at both you and your new spouse involved (even if months or years have transpired between your divorce and remarriage).

   c.) Because of bitterness and revenge, we have seen individuals attempt to divide their former spouse's family by allying with their former in-laws.

d.) Your former spouse may have had hopes of reconciling with you. If so, your remarriage has likely broken that dream and created additional hurt.

2. Jealousy can be a big factor. The fact that you have moved forward with your life can stir up deep feelings of envy in your former spouse.

   a.) Perhaps prior to your remarriage you and your former spouse were reasonably working things out regarding the children. Now that you are remarried, you may have had to change your approach or communication style with your former spouse so that your new spouse feels secure in your new marriage. As we stated earlier, your relationship with your new spouse has to take the highest place in your life, in order to make sure your spouse feels secure in your relationship.

   b.) A former spouse may sense that the new parent in your new home is trying to

   - take their place as the other biological parent, or
   - alienate their child from them, or
   - circumvent their parental relationship or authority.

   The biological parent/child bond is a precious thing, and when it is threatened by a new parent who is trying to bond with their new child (which is the right thing to do), the other biological parent may feel threatened by this activity. Such is the case when a biological parent objects to their child calling the new parent Mom or Dad.

   New parent/new child relationships need to be built in

your new home to build a healthy family. There needs to be effort to bond. Communication with the other biological parent and child is necessary to let them know that the new parent is in no way trying to replace the biological parent or take away any authority.

c.) The former spouse may disapprove, dislike, or disagree with your way of parenting or raising the children in your new home. There could be something you are doing that contradicts with their fundamental beliefs.

Children are often caught in the middle of strife between their biological parents. This can vary from custody battles to attendance of special events in the child's life. No matter what strife exists between former spouses, to their child they are still Mom and Dad. And because of the parent/child bond, the child usually only sees the best of each parent. The child does not see the broken promises and commitments, unpaid child support, or harsh words. The child is focused on their parents being at their special day.

While we encourage the prevention of others from bringing hurt and strife into our marriage and family, care should be given to our actions knowing that our children could likely suffer from once again being caught in the middle of the strife.

Realize that your child's other biological parent will likely be a part of your child's life (and therefore your life also) for years to come. So it is in your new family's best interest to attempt to develop an amicable relationship for the benefit of your children.

Realize that divorce and the mistakes people made that added to the ending former of relationships have created pain in many people.

Yes, we agree that when we repent, Jesus forgives us completely. Yet, we have to deal with consequences from our failures such as:

- Some people do not forgive. The hurt is still a part of them, and hurting people hurt other people—especially the ones who hurt them. (Some do forgive, but it may take years or another event in their life to forgive and move on.)
- Bitterness of soul will cause people to not see the hurt they are causing in other people's lives—including the lives of their own children.

## Typical Reactions that Do Not Work

We often react hastily to the trouble and strife caused by former spouses. The following reactions usually make matters worse:

- ignoring them,
- stubbornness,
- tit for tat; insult for insult,
- lashing out at them,
- aggression and arguing,
- pushing their "hot" buttons,
- threats,
- avoidance, and
- using the children.

## Solving Former Spouse Conflicts

Since we will likely continue to have former spouses in our lives for years to come, we need the grace of God to manage our relationships with them. Jesus taught the following in Luke 6:

*But I tell you who hear me: Love your enemies, do good to those who hate you, bless those who curse you, pray for those who mistreat you. If someone strikes you on one cheek, turn to him the other also. If someone takes your cloak, do not stop him from taking your tunic* (Luke 6:27–29).

This verse is most difficult to live, but there is a blessing in following it. In 2 Chronicles 28 the Kingdom of God was split and the two sides were at war with each other—like in many divorces. The army of Israel warred against Judah, capturing 200,000 women and children from Judah and seizing vast plunder, which they took back to Samaria. But a prophet of the Lord named Oded was there in Samaria when the army of Israel returned home. He went out to meet them.

*He (Oded) said to them, "Because the Lord, the God of your fathers, was angry with Judah, he gave them into your hand But you have slaughtered them in a rage that reaches to heaven. And now you intend to make the men and women of Judah and Jerusalem your slaves. But aren't you also guilty of sins against the LORD your God? Now listen to me! Send back your fellow countrymen you have taken as prisoners, for the Lord's fierce anger rests on you"* (2 Chronicles 28:9–11).

Then some of the leaders of Israel agreed with this and confronted the men returning from battle.

*"You must not bring the prisoners here!" they declared. "We cannot afford to add to our sins and guilt. Our guilt is already great, and the Lord's fierce anger is already turned against Israel"* (2 Chronicles 28:13).

So the warriors released the prisoners and handed over the plunder in the sight of the leaders and all the people. Then the men distributed clothes from the plunder to the prisoners who were naked. They provided clothing and sandals to wear, gave them enough food and drink, and dressed their wounds with olive oil. They put those who were weak on donkeys and took all the prisoners back to their own people in Jericho, the city of palms. Then they returned to Samaria.

The objective of this story is to point out how we are to treat others (sometimes our own family) who bring strife into our life, as Jesus spoke of in Luke 6. In your prayer time, ask the Holy Spirit what He would have you do for your former spouse. Then do what He tells you.

## Consider These Thoughts

*A former spouse is not our enemy—the devil is.*

Our adversary works through people to stir up trouble in our families. Our adversary looks for opportunities to use any of us to create division and strife in relationships. He may have found opportunity in the past to work through you when you reacted negatively to being threatened, or became selfish, rude, angry, critical, or fearful.

*Try to understand the one who is causing trouble.*

When someone is causing trouble in our lives, we become defensive, or even angry with them. We do not see any value in that person, and we do not want to let them off the hook. Remember what we have already learned.

1. Perhaps the one who offended you did not intend harm. Ask yourself if the comment or action was really meant as an

attack against you.

2. Hurting people hurt people, and are easily hurt by people. Perhaps the presence of hurt in your offender's life causes them to hurt you and others. Just knowing this will help you to deal with those people in a more constructive, positive way.
3. Are you easily hurt by people? Are you oversensitive about the words and actions of a former spouse? If you are still hurting from your past, you may become easily hurt by others.
4. Though a former spouse may be taking you to court, or not paying child support, or speaking negatively about you to your children or other family members, or in other ways trying to create strife in your life, God still loves that person as much as He loves you. Jesus paid the same great price to remove your offender's sins and your sins.

*We judge ourselves by our intentions, but we judge offenders by their actions.*

When we have hurt someone, we may be regretful and want to ask for forgiveness, saying that we did not mean to hurt them, our intentions were right. We want others to give us the "benefit of the doubt" for our actions. However, when someone has hurt us, their actions speak louder than their reasoning, and we usually hold them accountable. We distance ourselves from them, refusing to give them the benefit of the doubt.

*Communicate and consider an apology.*

If you and your new spouse can agree on this course of action, try talking to your former spouse about how and why they are being difficult. (You may already know why.) If they are reacting to pain in their life from the divorce, apologize to them for:

- your faults or actions that caused the former marriage to fail
- any hurt you have caused in their life

If your apology is sincere, it may go a long way to beginning a peaceful life in your new home.

*Pray for them.*

We know this can be tough to do, especially praying and asking God to bless someone who is creating strife and hardship, but following Jesus' command can do miracles. Pray for those people you may have hurt. Ask God to save them and heal them as only He can.

A few years ago we met a couple who had constantly dodged bullets (verbal attacks, insults, and strife) for seven years from her former spouse. During those years they prayed for God to bring peace between them, to remove the verbal abuse from him, or in other ways to make their new marriage and family peaceful.

When they were challenged to pray for his salvation and God's blessings on his life, they were skeptical that this prayer would work. But after only one week of praying this self-less prayer every day, the difficult former spouse called (not once, but twice in two consecutive days) to apologize for all of his bad behavior, and he even complimented her on how well she had done raising their children. It was truly a breakthrough and a miracle for her new family and her children.

The content of our prayer truly makes a difference. There are basically two types of prayers that people pray. The first type is self-centered prayer—to take care of our personal and family needs and desires.

The second type is self-less prayer—prayers of compassion for other people for God to bless, heal, save, and deliver them. There is power in a prayer that puts others' needs ahead of our own. This type prayer touches the heart of Christ who is moved by compassion for others.

Through self-less prayer, you can be a witness of God's unconditional love to a former spouse. If you have a relationship with Jesus, you have what they need to find eternal life and heal their hurts. We have shared this scripture twice before, but we repeat it because it applies to all of the people in your world:

> *The Spirit of the LORD is upon Me, because He has anointed Me to preach the gospel to the poor; He has sent Me to heal the brokenhearted, to proclaim liberty to the captives and recovery of sight to the blind, to set at liberty those who are oppressed; to proclaim the acceptable year of the LORD* (Luke 4:18).

Wow! What great love God our Father has for each of us—and for our former spouses—to send His Son to meet our every need. God just might want to use you to help them find His love and healing—what a thought! Pray for God to give you favor with them. God, grants us favor with men.

*Maintain control during conversations.*

Make your conversations with your former spouse brief and informative. If they try to start an argument, then end the conversation. They may resist this, but after a few times they will begin to realize that you will not engage their behavior.

Do not let your new spouse be your messenger between you and your former spouse. Doing so can irritate an already tense situation.

*Pick your battles, and be a peacemaker.*

Some issues are not worth a fight. It is better to work around some issues than to live in strife. Don't let your emotions engage you in a battle that will pay little dividends for your family. When I come home stressed, Paige becomes stressed. Our emotions are contagious and will infect all of our family members. Sometimes winning a battle is just not worth the strife that it brings. Do not let another person's negative emotions trigger the same in you. Maintain control of yourself, and your family. Let your contagious emotion be peace.

For example, if your struggle is over getting the children for a specific holiday, choose to celebrate the holiday on a different day—and enjoy a peaceful day. Be a peacemaker. Consider these two verses:

> *Blessed are the peacemakers, for they will be called sons of God* (Matthew 5: 9).

> *You're blessed when you can show people how to cooperate instead of compete or fight. That's when you discover who you really are, and your place in God's family* (Matthew 5:9 MSG).

Look at yourself—do you create difficulty in your former spouse's home? Remember that your children do not need to see their biological parents in strife. Do whatever is necessary to be a peacemaker, and minimize the strife. Take the high road. Do not let a person's negative action create your negative reaction.

### *Legal Recourse*

There are times when issues can only be settled through the legal system. When the other person is continually bringing harm to your family and will not reason with you, you must take the necessary steps to protect your family from negative outside influence. Whenever possible, be willing to compromise and work things out, but if necessary consult your attorney for advice.

### *Above all, walk in the character of Christ.*

The fruit of Christ's Spirit as found in Galatians 5:22–23 is love, joy, peace, patience, kindness, goodness, faithfulness, gentleness, and self-control.

Examine yourself and identify the fruit that is evident in your life. Now focus on the top two that you lack the most. Work on improving yourself in those areas. Lap-time with your Heavenly Father will increase the Spirit of Christ in you, and will change the things that you cannot change on your own.

## Our Prayer for You

Heavenly Father, we ask You to pour out Your love into and around this new family. Give every family member favor with all extended family involved. Let there be a spirit of acceptance, the same spirit by which You accept us into Your Kingdom. Help this couple to identify and successfully resolve any issue with an extended family member who is attempting to divide this new marriage, and to rebuild those relationships.

Help this family to heal wounds and build peace with their former spouses. Give them Your favor as a shield.

We thank You that a strong covenant relationship is ever increasing in this family, such that nothing can cause separation or tear it apart. We pray in Your Son's name. Amen.

## Not So Funny Family Moments

This does not represent a "funny" funny moment, but we are no respecter of children. At one point or another, we left one child at church, forgot to pick another up at school, and were late to get one from daycare on more than one occasion.

As parents, we are certainly not proud of those moments. On the contrary, we believe it was important for us to be early to pick up our children to show them they are important and they can depend on us. So we always strived to be early for our children. Children who have faced trauma of divorce or death of a parent need to feel secure. Being early for them is another step in building their trust in us.

We do look back and shake our heads in disappointment at ourselves for those moments.

## Chapter 9

# Purpose for Your Family

*Moe Becnel*

### *We All Fall Short: A Note to Children of Divorce*

*It's easy to dwell on the hurt and unfairness divorce brings, especially when you are just an innocent victim. I would just like to encourage you in moments when you feel the hurt and offense, and realize that it's never what God intended for you. We live in a broken world, and we all have (and will continue to) hurt loved ones in our life. This is where grace comes in. Grace is the unmerited, undeserved favor that God extends to us, and God asks us to extend the same to those around us. Forgive your parents, as Christ forgives you (see Ephesians 4:32).*

*Also, understand that parents hurt, too. It's not easy for them. They may have never wanted a divorce. Choosing to focus on the blessings brought from a difficult situation really helps me. I now have six awesome siblings, and my new parents are so dear and special to me. God never wastes a hurt.*

*The Bible tells us, "And we know that in all things God works for the good of those who love Him"(Romans 8:28).* —Melanie

■ ■ ■

ALL PEOPLE NEED a purpose for their lives other than simply meeting their needs and satisfying their own wants. Without future plans and goals, we will live a very unfulfilled life. Many marriages and families have crumbled because a couple did not have a common vision or purpose for the relationship. If each spouse stays focused on their own desires, struggles within the marriage will follow as each person battles to fulfill their ways and their wants.

The Bible describes man's need for a vision.

> *Where there is no revelation, the people cast off restraint . . .* (Proverbs 29:18a).

When God created you, He also created a specific plan and purpose for you. Self-help books that target helping people find their purpose have sold tens of millions of copies. This fact proves that people are searching for their purpose.

Unfortunately, many people search a lifetime for their purpose and never find it because they do not look to God, who created their life and their individual purpose. Even before you were born God knew where you would be today.

The Bible tells us that Father God has a detailed plan for you and your new Blended Family already laid out.

> *"For I know the plans I have for you," declares the LORD, "plans to prosper you and not to harm you, plans to give you hope and a future"* (Jeremiah 29:11).

God wants you to find His plan for your life and walk in it. If you do not know God's vision or goal for your life, your marriage or your family, ask Him in your prayer time to begin to show you.

Some progressive Christian churches have classes that help people find, develop, and begin to walk in their purpose. These classes help the individual understand God and His plan for them. They also help identify inherent God-given gifts, talents, and abilities.

Your purpose will always involve your God-given talents. We encourage you to seek your purpose. We also encourage parents to help their children find their purpose and begin to walk in it. The earlier the age the better.

## Planning

It's been said many times that people and businesses do not plan to fail, they fail to plan.

Consider the many New Year's resolutions made every January—resolutions to draw closer to God, to lose weight, to be a better person, to get out of debt, to start a new career, to learn a new language, and so on. Most of these resolutions are never accomplished. Why? Because no action plans are put in place to achieve them.

The first step in successful planning is writing down your vision and purpose. When God gives you a vision or shows you your purpose, write it down.

> *Write down the revelation and make it plain on tablets, so that a herald [or whoever reads it] may run with it* (Habakkuk 2:2).

At the beginning of each year, Paige and I had a habit of individually writing down goals and prayer requests—sort of a "wish list" of what we wanted God to do in our lives over the next year. For several years, the goals and requests remained individual and personal between God and each of us.

Then we decided to take the idea of taking goal setting a step further by coming together in agreement over goals for our family. If Paige and I were to become one, we needed to have a common vision and common goals. We knew what we wanted our family to believe in and become, but we had never written it down. We decided to write a mission statement—an idea I brought home from work—for our family.

A mission statement is a written declaration, usually one or two sentences, describing the goals and objectives of an entity (a business, church, organization, etc.). You can read the Blending A Family (BAF) Mission Statement on page 301 of this book.

Business executives know that their business cannot be everything to everyone, so they write mission statements describing what they want their business to become or accomplish, and to be successful at that. Each business executive team consciously decides where they will locate the store, what they want to be known for, and how they want to serve their customers, down to what warranties or return policies they offer.

For example, every grocery store chain is different. While most groceries today have a pharmacy and banking facilities within a store, some will have video movie rentals, another will offer dry cleaning service, while another will specialize in its elaborate deli or bakery. Some choose to have salad bars, enabling their customers to buy fresh salad by the pound. Others rent carpet shampoo equipment to customers. Some groceries focus on selling prime beef, fresh fish, or offering a huge wine selection.

Executives use their mission statement to develop the company's plans, strategies, and annual financial goals. If such a process helps companies achieve success, we concluded that it could help our family achieve success, too.

So one night our Blended Family sat around the kitchen table after dinner and developed a Becnel/Morriz Family Mission Statement that focused on relational and spiritual issues for our family. We allowed our children to participate in the process, asking what was important to them for our family to become and to accomplish.

It was very important that we allowed each child to have input into the family goals, as we realized later how it gave them a sense of belonging to the family, and ownership in the family goals. During the family meeting, I just took notes. Paige and I let everyone add something, and when everyone had commented we started around the table again; we went around the table three times giving our comments and asking for comments until everyone had no additional suggestions. We discussed things that we had enjoyed doing together as a family. All comments and ideas were considered valuable. Even though they were relatively young, our children actually got into the mode of expressing themselves, and giving their ideas. I also believe the process added value to them as they saw their thoughts being written down.

Then I took the list, grouped similar comments and developed a mission statement, making sure that each child could find something they said in our family mission statement. From that family meeting we developed the following mission statement:

*Becnel/Morriz Family Mission Statement*

The mission of the Becnel/Morriz family is
to serve Jesus Christ our Lord, as a family,
to express God's love, respect, honor and grace toward each other,
to respect and appreciate the individuality that God gave each of us,
to share the love we have for each other with those who need love,
encouragement, and hope, and to have fun!

The next step in the planning process is to establish a strategy for accomplishing your family's purpose outlined in the mission statement. Much of the strategy below came from the family meeting. Here is the mission statement strategy we developed:

*Strategy to Accomplish Our Mission Statement*

Each family member will:

- Pursue the character of Jesus in his or her life
- Establish a high moral standard
- Stand up for righteousness (right choices), wherever he or she is
- Abstain from R-rated or questionable movies and television programs
- Discipline with love and grace
- Treat each person in our family as equal
- Honor, respect, and appreciate each other
- Pray seven days for seven people—(Nicole made a chart of who we prayed for each day of the week and put it on our refrigerator door.)
- Be involved in our church

- Be involved in outreach to others in the community
- Enjoy vacations and other fun activities as a family

You and your spouse probably have goals, but have you ever discussed them or written them down? If so, have you determined the steps needed to accomplish your goals?

If you set a high standard of righteousness and excellence in your life and in your home with a strategy for achieving those standards, your family and children will reap great dividends.

We suggest the following key components be a part of your family's mission statement in some manner:

- Jesus as the center of the home, with the fruit of the Spirit in control

  *But the fruit of the spirit is love, joy, peace, patience, kindness, goodness, faithfulness, gentleness, and self-control* (Galatians 5:22–23).

- Pursuit of righteousness and holiness
- Love flowing within the family (spouse to spouse, parents to children, children to parents), in the same way that Father God and Jesus love each other
- Love flowing externally (involvement with others outside your family), in the same way that Jesus loves us
- What you want your children to learn
- Commitment to each other
- Unified dreams and desires
- Appreciation for each other
- Gratitude—focus on what you have, not what you lack

Mission statements can be written for a variety of topics. A family will likely have multiple goal categories, including spiritual, relational, educational, recreational, and financial goals. A mission statement for each of these areas can help define purpose and direction, bring agreement, and create harmony and unity within the family.

The mission statement can also help identify solutions to conflicts between the husband and wife, such as developing agreement on rules and discipline. In Chapter 3, we discussed potential divisions in a home. The process of sitting down and writing a mission statement will identify these divisions and help develop an action plan to eliminate them.

Writing a mission statement opens the lines of communication between spouses, and between parents and children. You may (or may not) be surprised to find that the goals of your spouse are different than your own. Exploring the differences can help you meld the two, and work toward common goals.

I know that writing a mission statement sounds like a crazy idea; I received a strange look from Paige the day I suggested it. But do not knock it until you try it. Make plans to develop your own family mission statement, and see what writing down goals and strategies will do to bring agreement and focus to building a healthy family.

## Our Prayer for You

Oh gracious Father, help this husband and wife to seek Your vision and purpose for their family. We know You have a supernatural purpose for them which will bring blessing to them first, and through them to others. Help each family member to honor and appreciate each other. Bless them today, and direct their steps into Your perfect will. Build their love for You and their love for each other. Be the Author and Finisher of their faith as You promise to do. We love You and thank You for being intricately involved in their lives. In Jesus' mighty name. Amen.

## Funny Family Moments

On a vacation to Washington DC and Virginia to visit Melanie, our eldest daughter, we drove to Virginia Beach for some beach time. It rained the two days we were there. So our "bored" children who love being on video decided to produce, direct, and star in their own cereal commercials with the boxes of cereal we had on hand. They each grabbed a box, sang the jingle, and made up a dance. We had as much fun watching as they had performing.

Chapter 10

# Prayer—An Awesome Thing

*Moe Becnel*

*I remember in the beginning of our new family developing, home wasn't always a peaceful place. It would get very heated in our household between my dad and my new mom, so heated at times it was very scary for me as a young child. The tense arguments were so loud and magnified to my ears it terrified me. I would think, "Here we go again," or even, "I don't want to get yelled at."*

*But it was through those tough times that my new older sister, Nicole, would gather us together, all the kids, and bring us up to her bedroom and hold us all real close. She knew what was happening more than the rest of us and, as we didn't understand what was happening, she would pray. Then she would keep telling us that we would be ok.*

*I remember it was prayer that got us through.*

*It was prayer that gave us peace.*

*It was prayer that gave us strength.*

*It was prayer that made the difference in my mind.* —Jordan

■ ■ ■

WE'VE SAVED THE BEST for last—prayer. Prayer is not the topic of the last chapter because it is the last resort. Rather, we know that people remember the last few things they hear or read. If you do not remember anything else from this book, you need to understand the amazing resource you have through communication with Father God through His Holy Spirit. Prayer is your lifeline to supernatural understanding, guidance, and power.

The power of prayer has been the sustaining force that brought the wisdom, the knowledge, the breakthrough and the victory in our lives and in our Blended Family. Prayer has been the overwhelming power that has produced the positive change in our hearts first, and then in our Blended Family. There were many days in our early years when Paige and I had no more emotional strength to continue trying to build our family. As Jordan stated above, the struggles were frequent and intense. We were ready to give up many times. But the non-denominational Christian church in which Paige and I met had given us a strong foundation in the power of prayer. We had been taught about spiritual warfare and, in spite of all the struggles of trying to build this new family, we knew that our fight was not against each other, against our children or even against our former spouses. Rather, it was mostly our adversary who was trying to divide us and our family. But when our negative emotions took over, we often reacted negatively against one another.

> *What causes fights and quarrels among you? Don't they come from your desires that battle within you? You want something but don't*

*get it. You kill and covet, but you cannot have what you want. You quarrel and fight. You do not have because you do not ask. When you ask, you do not receive, because you ask with wrong motives, that you may spend what you get on your pleasures* (James 4: 1–3).

We lack in areas of our lives because we do not ask for help in prayer, or because we ask for the wrong things and with selfish motives.

Christians so often underestimate the power of prayer. God is our ally. God is selfless and loving. He redeems us and calls us His children. We are heirs to all that belongs to God. Jesus called His disciples "friends." If you have accepted Jesus as your Savior and Lord and seek to follow Him, you are also His disciple. Today Jesus sits at the right hand of the throne of God and intercedes for you and me.

The real solution to conflicts between spouses or with other people is to retreat from attacking or blaming each other, and to advance in prayer and in God's Word against your adversary. You tap that incredible heavenly resource when you allow your prayer life and your personal life to intersect, presenting your daily personal life (issues, relationship breakdowns, decisions, meetings, and feelings) to God.

I intentionally repeat myself—God cherishes your new family! He wants to give you everything you need to build a loving Blended Family. But you will only hear from God and gain His instruction when you spend time in prayer communicating with Him and seeking His will for you, your spouse, your marriage, and all children.

We have given you many truths from God's Word to help you build your family. Yet, because your family is different from ours (different dynamics and personalities) you need to seek God's direction for applying those truths to your family.

## Prayer Initiates Positive Change

Insanity has been described as "doing the same thing over and over and expecting different results." The same is true of our prayer life. If we pray the same amount of time, with the same lack of zeal, with the same weak sacrifice and the same level of distraction, we cannot and will not experience positive change. If you need radical change in your life, your marriage, your new family, or your children, you need to radically change your approach to prayer.

All people resist change. It is difficult to break habits; multi-million dollar businesses thrive on this fact. Consider the money people spend in the stop smoking and weight-loss industries, all because they are not able to change by themselves. These people have become slaves to their habits, and now lack self-discipline or will power.

Because it is so difficult to change, we would rather try to change those around us, including our spouse and children, than change ourselves. We usually pray for God to change our circumstances or a troublesome child or former spouse, rather than praying for God to change us.

Unfortunately, in order to solve our problems, God most often needs to change us. And the change almost always calls for more of the character of Jesus to become manifest in our lives—more love, more compassion, more servanthood, more mercy, more grace, more holiness, more humility, less pride, less want, and less self.

You can initiate positive change in your life, and you do not have to do it alone. Your loving Father, the Almighty Creator of the universe and the detailed planner of your life, wants to help you. Just ask God in your prayer time with a sincere heart, and be willing to change your heart.

For people to initiate a change in their life, they must want the change. And they will only want the change when they see enough value in making it. In Luke 11:2–4, Jesus taught His disciples how to pray; He gave them the "Our Father," which outlines the elements of . . .

- worship,
- praise,
- thanksgiving,
- prayer requests,
- forgiveness, and
- protection.

In Jesus' next statement in Luke 11, He tells His disciples why they should pray, showing them the value of prayer.

> *Then he said to them, "Suppose one of you has a friend, and he goes to him at midnight and says, 'Friend, lend me three loaves of bread, because a friend of mine on a journey has come to me, and I have nothing to set before him.'*
>
> *"Then the one inside answers, 'Don't bother me. The door is already locked, and my children are with me in bed. I can't get up and give you anything.'*
>
> *"I tell you, though he will not get up and give him the bread because he is his friend, yet because of the man's boldness he will get up and give him as much as he needs.*
>
> *"So I say to you: Ask and it will be given to you; seek and you will find; knock and the door will be opened to you. For everyone who asks receives; he who seeks finds; and to him who knocks, the door will be opened.*
>
> *"Which of you fathers, if your son asks for a fish, will give him*

> *a snake instead? Or if he asks for an egg, will give him a scorpion? If you then, though you are evil, know how to give good gifts to your children, how much more will your Father in heaven give the Holy Spirit to those who ask Him"* (Luke 11:5–13).

Jesus knew human nature. He knew the disciples had to understand the benefit and the power that comes from prayer before they would make prayer a permanent part of their lives. Once you realize the power in prayer, prayer will become a vital part of your life.

## How Prayer Works

As we pray for a person or an issue, we get a "new view." We begin to see the person or issue through the eyes of the Holy Spirit.

This "new view" creates a "new heart" or "new knowledge" in us. We develop a heart of compassion for that person, or a heart of understanding about the issue.

The "new heart" moves us to "new actions." We begin to treat that person differently, taking the high road, extending grace, or we respond differently to the issue.

The "new actions" cause "new reactions" from others. People will often change in response to our consistent new actions, or the new actions become a positive step to resolve the issue. True, unconditional love always brings forth a response, and God's wisdom leads to success.

> *As the heavens are higher than the earth, so are my ways higher than your ways and my thoughts than your thoughts* (Isaiah 55:9).

As we pray we find God's view, God's thoughts, and God's wisdom to solve our problems and grow our relationships.

## Circle of Influence

Below is a bull's eye with three circles (inner, middle and outer). Within the inner circle is *your family*.

In the middle circle write down things that you and your spouse have control over, such as where you live, the car you drive, your financial spending, your thoughts, your tongue (words), etc. List about ten more.

In the outer circle, write down what and whom you cannot control, such as the economy, the weather, the cat, your former spouse, etc. List about ten others.

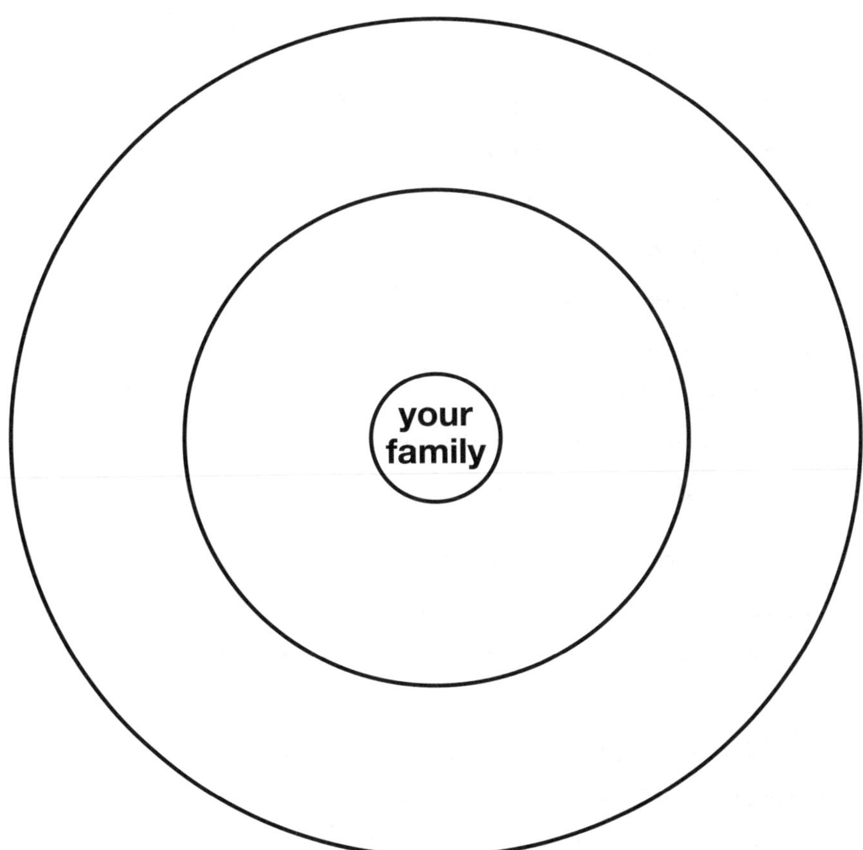

The point of this exercise is twofold. First, we want you to visualize that there are things both in your control and out of your control that affect your family. Second, because we are in covenant with Almighty God, His loving kindness works on our behalf on the things we have no control over. In the Old and New Testaments, the power of God worked on man's behalf to part the sea, tear down walls, rebuild walls, heal the sick, raise the dead, calm the storms, and restore dreams. Fervent (intense) prayer for the people and issues in your outer circle will change your life . . . if you do not doubt.

> *Early in the morning, as He [Jesus] was on His way back to the city, He was hungry. Seeing a fig tree by the road, He went up to it but found nothing on it except leaves. Then He said to it, "May you never bear fruit again!" Immediately the tree withered. When the disciples saw this, they were amazed. "How did the fig tree wither so quickly?" they asked.*
>
> *Jesus replied, "I tell you the truth, if you have faith and do not doubt, not only can you do what was done to the fig tree, but also you can say to this mountain, 'Go, throw yourself into the sea,' and it will be done. If you believe, you will receive whatever you ask for in prayer"* (Matthew 21:18–21).

Nothing is impossible with God! But our prayer needs to be selfless, and in accordance with His Will for us and for our family. And we must have faith that God is for us, and His Word is truth.

## Honor God's Words—Write them Down

The Bible is God's Word, written by men who were under the inspiration of the Holy Spirit. There are some philosophers who say the Bible is not the only Word of God, it is not relevant today, or in other ways discount His Word.

Our family has done our best to trust in and apply God's principles found throughout the Bible. We have seen the success in our family that comes from doing things God's way. There are two very important things to consider for your successful life.

First, God's principles found in His Word are commands, not suggestions. We are to be obedient to God and His ways. When you "digest" His principles, you are blessed. What you build your home on will be tested by wind and fire. There are many homes in which live people who confess Jesus as their Savior, but they have not built their home on God's foundation. The floors of their marriages have cracks and the walls are unstable. When you ignore God's Word you are telling Him that He does not know as much as you do. In essence, you are your own god.

Second, prayer is a two-way communication with God. It should consist of us praising, thanking, and petitioning God, and God speaking to us. In your quiet time in prayer the Holy Spirit (your Counselor and Guide) will speak to your thoughts and give you direction. He will show you flaws in your life, marriage, family, finances, and business; He will guide you to correct them.

Those words you hear in your thoughts from His Spirit are as much the Word of God as what the writers of the Bible wrote. Therefore, every word of guidance the Holy Spirit speaks to you is worth writing down. Take a notebook and pen to prayer with you and write what you hear. Check it to make sure it agrees with the Bible (sometimes we hear our own self-centered thoughts). Then do what He tells you to do.

## Your Altar

An altar represents the place where God and man meet. Many times in the Old Testament, men built altars to God to honor and express their gratitude and devotion to Him.

Jesus brought us a new way. With His New Covenant He placed His Spirit within us. Although we no longer have to make animal sacrifices to God, we still have responsibility to God . . .

- to build our altar—that place where we meet God daily. Designating a special place for prayer shows *honor* to God.
- to stay at the altar—to give God our heart and life, and to follow Him daily.

Prioritize your life so that prayer does not get pushed off your agenda.

> *But seek first His kingdom and His righteousness [right choices in your life], and all these things [whatever you need] will be given to you as well* (Matthew 6:33).

As we stated before, if you need change in your life or family, you have to change your prayer life—your devotion.

## Hold Your Family Up in Prayer

Paige and I were shocked when we read Jordan's story above; we were unaware that we had created so much more additional hurt in our children. After nineteen years into our marriage and family, we learned that Nicole had taken on the role of "protector" to her brother and sisters. We thank God that Paige and others had instilled the power of prayer in Nicole's heart years ago. Recall in the previous chapter that Nicole was our child who added to our Family Mission Statement, "Pray seven days for seven people." Nicole made a chart of whom we prayed for each day and put it on our refrigerator door.

As you can see, prayer will even brings positive results in children. A person is never too young to learn to communicate and fellowship with their Heavenly Father. The *boy* Joshua grew up as an assistant to Moses and he stayed in the presence of God. The *boy* Samuel grew up as an apprentice under the prophet Eli and lived in the Temple. At the age of twelve, Jesus was spending time in the Temple on His own.

There is no reason why your children cannot pray with you or for you. They will learn to pray by hearing you and others pray. They will learn to pray by praying. We exposed our children to prayer at an early age. Before I met Paige, she would take her girls to 6:00am morning prayer at the church one to two days each week. After we were married, we attended prayer meetings, to which we brought our children and expected them to pray, though we did not expect them to pray for long periods of time. We prayed with our children in the car each morning during our drive to school.

As a result, I have seen our family knit together more through prayer with and for each other (and for their friends) than in anything else we could ever have done.

Our children will also testify to the power of prayer. In 1999, Paige and I took all of our children and one of our sons-in-law on a seven-day cruise in the Caribbean. Melanie, our oldest married daughter, was four months pregnant and had a terrible bout of sea-sickness. Our daughter Kristen suggested we pray for her. In the middle of a crowd on a snorkeling boat our family knelt beside her, encircled and laid hands on her, and prayed. It wasn't too long before she was feeling well enough to enjoy the rest of the trip.

Mom and Dad, you must set the example. When your children see how important prayer is to you, it becomes important to them. When they are included as a vital part of those prayers and see it change lives, they will learn to respect its power.

Husbands and wives should continually hold each other and their children up in prayer. Pray for all areas of your children's lives, including for healing from the pain of divorce or death of a parent, for godly friends, for success in school, for purity, for spiritual growth, for fruit of the Spirit of God (see Galatians 5:22–23), for godly future spouses, for dedication to God's ministry, and for taking authority over the spirits of rebellion, disobedience, strife, peer pressure, and manipulation. In prayer, ask God to help each child feel a part of your new family.

Set goals concerning prayer for your family. Consider these:

- Prepare your prayer each day—do not pray the same prayers day after day.
- Join a prayer meeting or attend prayer at church with your family.
- Set your alarm clock. Get up early to spend time with God.
- Pray specific prayers for each child's specific needs and future.
- Ask you children what they want to pray for, and encourage them to pray.

## Evaluate Your Prayer Life

Since prayer is vital to your spiritual health and your family's health and success, how would you rate your prayer life? Would you say it is *dynamic*, or maybe *effective*, or *weak*, or perhaps *non-existent*? Well if you are not sure, let us help. Consider the following categories, and rate yourself. Score yourself on a 1 to 5 scale (1 = poor, 5 = excellent) for each of the following four elements of prayer:

- Quantity: This is the amount of time you set aside to personally focus and converse with God. There are 1,440 minutes in each day. Assuming you sleep eight hours, you have 960 productive minutes each day. Giving God sixty focused minutes will truly change your life, and it will make the remaining 900 minutes so much more productive and successful.

  Before you say you do not have time, let me say that we always make time for what is important to us. It is a priority factor, not a time factor. It amazes me how much time I have when I turn off the TV and pick up God's Word or another book that helps me grow spiritually. If you want to know what you truly value in life, look where you spend your time.
- Quality: Is your prayer time focused, or is it filled with distractions? Take control of your thoughts and other distractions. Find a quiet place. Have effective conversation with God, praying for different people and needs each day. Do not repeat the same things day after day to God. Remember that Jesus is your best friend. If you repeated the same thing to the people you know day after day, they would surely not enjoy your company.
- Worship and Thanks: The great creator God is worthy of your worship and honor. Always give God thanks for who He is, what He has done for you, what He has given you, what He is going to do, and the people in your family. Thank Him often for sending Jesus to save you and for His Spirit to help you.
- Silence and Listening: Prayer is two-way communication. God wants to say some things to you. Have paper (a journal) and pen

ready to write what He tells you for your life and family. Block out all distractions, close your eyes, remain silent before God for at least ten full minutes, and listen in your thoughts.

From these four elements, identify where your weakest areas are, and focus to strengthen those areas. You will be amazed at your growth in doing this. As you make an effort to improve your prayer life, the effectiveness of your prayer (your prayers are getting answered) will surely change, your faith in God will increase, and you will grow in the reality of just how close your Father really is to you.

## Our Prayer for You

Father God, we know that Your Spirit has to draw man to you. We pray that You draw this family to You in a supernatural way. Give them a hunger for You, Your Word and Your Ways. Help them to change their priorities to put You first.

Speak Your Word into their hearts. Show them Your love, mercy, grace, and power by transforming their hearts first, and then their family. Breathe on each heart and create new life in their midst. We love you Father and we proclaim Jesus Lord! Amen.

# Epilogue

*Moe Becnel*

PAIGE AND I HAVE SHARED our hearts, our struggles, our failures and our successes with you. The success of our family is not a coincidence. We proved that doing things according to our way of reasoning led to failure, and a God-centered approach brought the positive change and blessing.

People have asked us, "Which of the Twelve Fundamentals are the most important?" Our answer is, "All of them!" All twelve truths work together like spokes on a bicycle wheel that give support to the wheel and keep the wheel round. You can work on one or two of the fundamentals at a time, but you cannot ignore the rest of them because all twelve fundamentals work together to build and unify your new family. I can explain it best this way. If you asked a mechanic to list the top three components that make an automobile mechanically sound, he would tell you, "All of them!"

The engine, steering wheel, accelerator peddle, engine oil, oil filter, cooling system, transmission, axles, wheel bearings, break peddle, tires, rims, wheel hubs, break linings, and every other component are equally essential to make the automobile work properly.

There are no shortcuts to building a high-quality car, and there are no shortcuts to building a loving, secure Blended Family.

I tell you now that blending a family isn't easy, and it doesn't happen quickly. Following are a few things we have learned about the process:

- It requires sacrifice. Ouch! We all hate that word.
- It requires patience—another tough one.
- It requires considering all those around you, even children, as more important than yourself.
- It requires an adoptive spirit—a heart of acceptance, which God will provide when you ask.
- It requires extending grace—treating others as God treats you.
- It requires setting goals and guidelines for yourself and your family.
- It requires a positive attitude. Do not expect others' attitudes to change until yours does.
- It requires prayer. God's voice and guidance come as we spend time communicating with Him.
- It requires faith (trust) that God will breathe on your Blended Family.

Becoming a loving Blended Family requires much from you, Mom and Dad. It is an investment into your future and your children's futures—knowing the dividends are great!

Years ago, I was going through a painful divorce, one which I did not want. I cried out to God, and told Him that I was determined to see a blessing come from this divorce. Twenty-two years later, here I am with my best friend, rewriting a book about the restoration and success that God has brought to us and to our children, and to many other Blended Families. Wow!

*Do not give up!* Never give up because of prolonged issues or circumstances. Admiral Jim Stockdale, the highest ranking United States military officer in the "Hanoi Hilton" prisoner of war (POW) camp during the height of the Vietnam War, was tortured over twenty times during his eight year imprisonment from 1965 to1973. Stockdale lived those eight years with no prisoner's rights, no set date to be freed, and no certainty of his future. During those eight years he provided leadership to the other prisoners under extreme adverse conditions, teaching the prisoners techniques to survive torture, developing an internal nonverbal communications system, and being an example of steadfastness in the midst of extreme and intense adversity.

How did he survive the POW camp until the end of the War and live a great life thereafter? Admiral Stockdale stated in an interview:

> "I never lost faith . . . I never doubted not only that I would get out, but also that I would prevail in the end and turn the experience into the defining event of my life, which, in retrospect, I would not trade."[1]

Admiral Stockdale had two principles he lived by. First, he faced the brutal facts of his situation and, second, he maintained faith that he would prevail in the end. He went on to say:

> "This is a very important lesson. You must never confuse faith that you will prevail in the end—which you can never afford to lose—with the discipline to confront the most brutal facts of your current reality, whatever they might be."[2]

---

[1, 2] Jim Collins, *Good to Great* (New York: Harper Collins Publishers, Inc. 2001) p85.

You, too, can make it through whatever challenges you and your family are facing. You can—and need to—be the steadfastness and encouragement that your family members need. Trust in God your Father, and you will not be disappointed. No matter what has happened in your past, or is happening now within your new family, God has a plan to bring a breakthrough for you into abundant life. We pray that you and your Blended Family will become and will achieve all that God desires for you, which is far above what you could ever imagine.

Stay close to the heartbeat of God—He will strengthen you and guide you.

God, your Creator and Father, is breathtaking and life giving.

Almighty God is on your side.

Appendix A

# God's Love and Plan for You

WHO IS THE MOST loving person you know? (Dogs don't count, though we can learn from them.) Is it your mother, a co-worker, a sibling, an aunt, a grandmother, a neighbor, a teacher, or someone at church?

Now think about that loving person's character. What made them so loving? They likely possess one or more of these traits:

- kindness
- thoughtfulness
- caring
- patience
- acceptance
- a positive attitude

## God's Unconditional Love

God loves you *infinitely* more than any person can. He is the epitome of unconditional love. What is God's unconditional love? A glimpse is found in 1 Corinthians 13. Read it slowly.

> *Love is patient, love is kind. It does not envy, it does not boast, it is not proud. It is not rude, it is not self-seeking, it is not*

*easily angered, and it keeps no record of wrongs. Love does not delight in evil but rejoices with the truth. It always protects, always trusts, always hopes, always perseveres. Love never fails.* (1Corinthians 13:4–8).

Wow! Wouldn't it be great to be loved like that? ? You are loved that way. God's love for you is immeasurable.

- He is no respecter of persons. He loves you the same as He does everyone else, no matter what you have done in your past (see Acts 10: 34).
- God keeps no record of wrongs (see 1Corinthians 13:5).
- He is patient and long-suffering with you (see 1Corinthians 13:4,7).
- His love never stops. He never quits or gives up on you (see 1Corinthians 13:8).
- He desires to heal the hurting, and restore the broken (see Isaiah 61:1–3).
- He has created a plan and destiny for you (see Jeremiah 29:11).

## Relationship with God

In the same way that a loving parent longs to be close to their child, Father God longs for intimate fellowship with you. We call it "lap-time," like when your child climbs in your lap or cuddles just to be close to you. *God wants that same kind of close relationship with you.* He wants to love on you, raise you, coach you, counsel you, advise you, and guide you in all areas of your life. He wants to protect you from making mistakes in life that will cause you and others pain.

## Christ—God's Greatest Love Gift

If you are like Paige, you may search through many stores at Christmas time, looking for that unique, perfect gift for a special loved one. Many times, after hours of searching, we find that perfect gift for that special person. We know it when we see it.

Because of sin, man was separated from our Heavenly Father. Our Father searched heaven for the most valuable gift to give us. Jesus, the only begotten Son of God, was the ultimate gift to you to redeem you back to Father God. Jesus became once-and-for-all the "Lamb of God who takes away the sins of the world"—your sins and mine (see John 1:29).

> *For God so loved the world that He gave His one and only Son, that whoever believes in Him shall not perish but have eternal life* (John 3:16).

> *To those who believe and receive His only begotten Son, Jesus Christ, God adopts us as sons and daughters* (2 Corinthians 6:18).

Even today, (2000 years later), these truths remain:

- God offers you His unconditional love—no matter what you have done.
- God is very approachable, and is waiting for you to sit with Him.
- When we repent and ask forgiveness of our sins, God remembers them no more.
- Jesus is at the right hand of the Father, making intercession (praying) for you.

## Prayer of Salvation

If you are ready to have that close relationship to God, the first step is accepting Jesus Christ as your personal Savior and Lord. Consider what the Bible says.

> *. . . for all have sinned and fall short of the glory of God* (Romans 3:23).

When you accept Christ, you acknowledge that you are in need of God's forgiveness.

> *For the wages of sin is death, but the gift of God is eternal life in Jesus Christ our Lord* (Romans 6:23).

When you accept Christ, you believe by faith and trust in Christ that eternal life is yours. You are a new creation. Your old life is gone, and your new life in Christ begins.

> *That if you confess with your mouth, "Jesus is Lord," and believe in your heart that God raised him from the dead, you will be saved. For it is with your heart that you believe and are justified, and it is with your mouth that you confess and are saved* (Romans 10:9–10).

Salvation is God's gift to you—you cannot earn it through good deeds. God simply waits for you to receive it by believing in Jesus and confessing Him as Lord.

If you are ready to receive Jesus into your heart and life, pray this prayer from your heart right where you are:

"Father God, I believe Your Word that I am a sinner and am in need of a savior. I am unable to work my way into heaven. I accept Your Son Jesus as my Savior and Lord of my life.

"Jesus, I ask you to come into my heart, cleanse me and make me new. Live in me and take control of my life. Help me to follow You and serve You all of my days. In Jesus name. Amen."

## Next Steps

Praise God—if you just prayed that prayer, the Bible says that the angels in heaven are singing and praising God for your redemption. What do you do now?

1. Find and attend a Christian church that challenges you to grow in the knowledge of God's Word.
2. Spend that lap-time with God daily, reading God's Word, talking to Him as friends do, and following Him.
3. Be baptized in water according to Jesus' command.
4. Serve others through your church, and allow the love of God to flow through you to others.

## Appendix B

# Mirror-Mirror on the Wall

THERE ARE MANY remarried spouses that are struggling to make their life and family a success. A part of the struggle is that family members are carrying baggage—hurts, failures, disappointments, negative feelings, bitterness, unforgiveness, negative attitudes, and/or bad habits from their past into their present.

Today we want to help you take a *real* look at yourself, to identify any negative behaviors you may have that may have contributed to, or caused previous failed relationships. The self-examination process is painful, but necessary so that you will have success in your future relationships.

We are *not* attempting to place one hundred percent blame on you for your previous failed relationships. Yet, it is necessary for you to determine any negative effect your attitudes, thoughts, actions or reactions may have had on your relationships.

### Our Experience

Moe experienced separation and divorce when his wife left him in 1987. He wanted no part of the divorce, and tried to reconcile over the next several months to save his marriage and family. As he shared his situation with others, he repeatedly told people, "My wife left *me*!"

One day while in prayer, God uttered these words to his thoughts, "Yes, your wife left you, but you are the one who made her *want* to leave." Ouch! That really hurt, because he did not realize the damage, or the extent of the damage, that he had done to the relationship—in part causing it to fail.

We believe the number one reason relationships fail is selfishness. A self-serving heart creates inappropriate attitudes, behaviors, actions, and words; the reactions from the spouse are often equally inappropriate.

## Snow White's Mirror

In the fable of Snow White, we hear the wicked queen repeatedly ask the mirror, "Mirror, mirror on the wall, who is the fairest of them all?" When the mirror would answer, "Snow White," the queen would become angry. She was looking at her own reflection, but not accepting the *truth* that it foretold. The queen could not see her own faults; she only saw Snow White as a competitor who was stealing her glory. Her response was to try to remove Snow White from her life, rather than determining why she (the queen) was not the fairest.

As humans, we have the same tendencies. We point fingers at others. We blame others for our failures. We want to remove people who have hurt us from our life. In Genesis 3:6–13, we read the account of Adam and Eve disobeying God's command to not eat fruit from a certain tree. In verses 12 and 13, we see Adam blame God for giving him Eve and blaming Eve for disobeying, and we see Eve blaming the serpent for deceiving her. Blame, blame, blame!

*And why do you look at the speck in your brother's eye, but do not consider the plank in your own eye? Or how can you say to your brother, 'Let me remove the speck from your eye'; and look, a plank is in your own eye? Hypocrite! First remove the plank from your own eye, and then you will see clearly to remove the speck from your brother's eye"* (Matthew 7:3–5).

Failing to look at yourself will cause additional failures in your relationships. Pointing a finger at others keeps you from evaluating your own internal shortcomings. We evaluate and criticize others in an effort to avoid evaluating ourselves.

## Self-Examination Process

Let's go through the following process of self-evaluation:

I. Identify Your Shortcomings

Self-inventory is tough, because the truth often hurts. But it is necessary so that you can identify and stop negative behaviors and attitudes that hurt others and damage relationships. Kind David, who was highly favored of God, wrote the following:

*Search me O God, and know my heart; test me and know my thoughts. Point out anything in me that offends You, and lead me along the path of everlasting life* (Psalm 139:23–24).

Wow—that is a bold prayer of self-examination. David asked God to "show him" because he knew he may be unaware of his own faults, just as the queen in Snow White and Adam & Eve were unaware of their own faults.

Are you willing to examine yourself? Say, "Yes!"

Okay, ask yourself these twenty-one questions. Give thought to each question. Be honest with yourself and with God (God already knows the answers).

1. Was God at the center of your marriage? (Psalm 127:1 reads, *Unless the Lord builds the house, they labor in vain who build it . . . .*)
2. What makes you truly happy?
3. What makes you unhappy?
4. Are you difficult to please? (Do you want things your way; do you want more material possessions; do other people's decisions always seem wrong to you; would you rather do things yourself, etc.)
5. Do you criticize your former spouse, or others? (A critical attitude will affect every person in your life.)
6. Do you gossip about your former spouse to others, complaining about him or her?
7. Did you try to change your former spouse when you were married to him or her? (Only God can change the heart of a man or woman—I'm sure you know that by now.)
8. Are you easily angered?
9. Have you used anger, pouting or stubbornness to get people to do what you want? (This is manipulation.)
10. Who was your best friend in your former marriage—your spouse, parent or other friend? (Your spouse needs to be your best friend.)
11. Were you more devoted to others (including your children), to a career, or to a hobby than to your former spouse?
12. Were you unfaithful to your former spouse (through adultery, pornography, chat rooms, etc.)?
13. Were you verbally abusive to your former spouse, putting them down instead of lifting them up?

14. Were you physically abusive to your former spouse?
15. How did you handle a bad decision made by your former spouse—emotionally or prayerfully? (Every person on earth will make mistakes.)
16. Were you a financial burden (excessive spender) or blessing (contributor, or managed resources well) to your former marriage?
17. Did your former spouse not meet your expectations? (When you expect things from other people, you set yourself up for disappointment. Set others free from your expectations, and let God to be your provider.)
18. Did you serve your former spouse and family, or your own interests and wants?
19. Can you truly forgive someone who hurt or offended you? (Forgiveness is vital to all life-long relationships. God requires us to forgive others.)
20. Have you asked God to show you any other areas that you may have missed? (See Psalm 139:23–24.)
21. Of all the characteristics of Jesus Christ found in Galatians 5:22–23 (love, joy, peace, longsuffering patience, kindness, goodness, faithfulness, gentleness and self-control), which do you lack the most?

II. Repent of Your Shortcomings

If you have identified some shortcomings, do not feel defeated or guilty. Some of your negative attitudes, harmful personality traits, and bad habits may stem back to your parents, your home environment, or an experience you had when you were growing up.

*Repent* means "such sorrow for past life as produces a new life." Never say, "That's just the way I am." You *can* change, and you need to change so you will have successful relationships.

1. Accept responsibility for your part of the damage done to your former marriage or relationships. Stop pointing fingers.
2. Ask God to forgive you for damaging your former relationships.

   *If we confess our sins, He is faithful to forgive us our sins and to cleanse us from all unrighteousness* (1John 1:9).

3 Now that God has forgiven you, forgive yourself.

   *There is therefore now no condemnation to those who are in Christ Jesus, who do not walk according to the flesh, but according to the Spirit* (Romans 8:1).

   Do not live with guilt. Guilt is not from God.

4. Forgive your former spouse for the part he or she played in causing the relationship to fail.
5. If you are remarried, commit to God and your new spouse to make positive change in your heart and your actions. Stop doing those things you identified that damage relationships.
6. Purpose in your heart that your new marriage will last a lifetime. Never give up. Never quit.

III. Look Forward

God has a plan for you and your new family.

> *"For I know the plans I have for you," declares the LORD, "plans to prosper you and not to harm you, plans to give you hope and a future"* (Jeremiah 29:11).

You may have *had* a failure, but *you* are not a failure. God is not mad at you. When we truly repent (change), God forgives and forgets. Your slate is clean. God loves you and your new family, and He wants it to last a lifetime. You get a "do-over" in real life. God's plan allows you to be a victor, not a victim. Go forth in God!

Appendix C

# Vows to Your New Children —It's Never Too Late

IN CHAPTER 6 we encourage new parents to share vows with their new children and presented the benefits of doing so. We recommend sharing vows during the wedding, or planning a special event if you are already remarried.

## Should Your Children Share Vows?

Some people have asked if it is appropriate for the children to share vows with the new parent. That depends on the children. If the children are showing signs of resistance, we suggest not. We believe that expecting a child to make vows to an adult, parent-figure that they did not choose to be a part of their life can put pressure on the child. We need to remember that the child did not request the marriage. *Let's let children be children, and let the adults take the responsibility for building the family.*

However, if the children are excited about the wedding and marriage, allowing them to also share vows to the new parents would be acceptable. You may want to ask the children their feelings about doing so, and not force them to do something they are uncomfortable with.

## Need a Great Sample Vow?

Brian and Ashley VanDreumel, good friends of ours and members of our church, allowed us to print the following vows that they wrote and shared with each other's children on their wedding day. (We had the privilege of officiating the VanDreumel's wedding.)

Brian and Ashley each stooped down and looked the children straight in the eyes as they spoke these vows into their new children's lives:

> *Brian:* "[Children's names], I want you to know that I dearly love your mother. We have become very good friends over the weeks and months and we have learned to love each other. As you have so graciously shared this wonderful woman with me, so will I share the love I feel for her with you. Together, we will learn much more about each other. I promise also to be fair and to be honest, to be available for you as I am for your mom, and in due time to earn your love, respect and true friendship. I will not attempt to replace anyone, but to make a place in your hearts that is for me alone. I will be father and friend, and I will cherish my life with all of you. On this day when I marry your mom, I marry you, and I promise to love and support you as my own."

> *Ashley:* "[Children's names], I want you to know that I dearly love your father. We have become very good friends over the weeks and months and we have learned to love each other. As you have so graciously shared this wonderful man with me, so will I share the love I feel for him with both of you. Together, we will learn much more about each other. I promise also to

be fair and to be honest, to be available for you as I am for your dad, and in due time to earn your love, respect and true friendship. I will not attempt to replace anyone, but to make a place in your hearts that is for me alone. I will be mother and friend, and I will cherish my life with both of you. On this day when I marry your dad, I marry you, and I promise to love and support you as my own."

The VanDreumel's children then responded to the following vows when read by the pastor:

*Pastor:* "[Children's names], do you promise to love your mother and her new husband?

*Children respond:* "I do."

*Pastor:* "Do you promise to support their marriage and your new family?"

*Children respond:* "I do."

*Pastor:* "Do you promise to accept the responsibility of being their children, and to encourage them, support them, and accept them just as our heavenly Father accepts us?"

*Children respond:* "I do."

*Pastor:* "[Children's names], do you promise to love your father and his new wife?

*Children respond:* "I do."

*Pastor:* "Do you promise to support their
marriage and your new family?"

*Children respond:* "I do."

*Pastor:* "Do you promise to accept the responsibility of being their children, and to encourage them, support them, and accept them just as our heavenly Father accepts us?"

*Children respond:* "I do."

There were not many dry eyes in the wedding hall when they finished.

We hope our sharing part of Brian and Ashley's wedding ceremony helps you understand the great value that children's vows can play in laying a foundation on which to build your family. Start planning how you will make sharing children's vows in your family a special event. Then watch the attitudes of all involved begin to change.

*Special thanks to Brian and Ashley for letting us share their vows with the world.*

Appendix D

# Resolving Conflicts in Families

EVERYONE EXPERIENCES CONFLICTS at different times. You may have had conflicts at your job, with creditors, with businesses, and even with people at church. Yet, the most devastating conflicts are found in families. Conflicts directly oppose the real purpose of a family. As long as a conflict is not properly resolved, the family and all family members suffer.

## Understanding Conflicts

In order to lay the foundation for resolving conflicts in relationships, it is helpful to understand the meaning of several terms.

The word *conflict* means "a fighting or struggle for mastery; a striving to oppose or overcome." Thus, conflicts involve a struggle created by opposing views, opinions, desires or purposes.

The word *resolve* means "to do away with doubts or disputes; to clear of difficulties."

And the word *resolution* is defined as "the act of unraveling a perplexing question or problem."

## Personal Conflict

Every day we face struggles within what our flesh wants versus what God's Spirit desires for our lives. The struggle between our flesh and God's Spirit is described in the Holy Bible as "the lust of the flesh, the lust of the eye, and the pride of life" (see 1 John 2:16).

## Relationship Conflict

> *What causes fights and quarrels among you? Don't they come from your desires that battle within you? You want something but don't get it. You kill and covet, but you cannot have what you want. You quarrel and fight. You do not have because you do not ask. When you ask, you do not receive, because you ask with wrong motives, that you may spend what you get on your pleasures* (James 4:1–3).

One of the toughest situations you may face is when two people you love are in conflict with each other, and you are in the middle. Children of divorce know this situation well, as divorced parents are often in conflict with each other. Extended family can create similar situations.

We believe that true conflict resolution is neither an art, nor is it a learned skill. *Rather, conflict resolution is an attitude of the heart.*

## Eleven Key Ingredients to Successful Conflict Resolution

1. Relationships are of utmost value.

God is all about life-long relationships. All Ten Commandments from God dealt with relationships. The first four discuss our relationship with God. The other six discuss our relationships with people. All other issues and decisions are important, but they are secondary to God.

As Christians, we are to pursue the heart of God and place great value on relationships. The relationship is always more important than any issue being discussed. Do not determine to win a conflict at the expense of damaging fellowship with that person. Always maintain respect for each other.

2. Change your perspective.

Value the other person, their feelings, their situation and their ideas. Your opinion or solution is not always the only good solution. Be open to accepting the other person's situations or ideas.

When the adulteress was brought to Jesus in John Chapter 8, Jesus was expected to condemn her. Jesus resolved a conflict between the woman needing forgiveness and her accusers. He successfully resolved the conflict by changing her accusers' perspective. He made them realize that they also had faults in their lives.

3. Never discuss a conflict when emotions are high.

Calm down first.

*My dear brothers, take note of this: Everyone should be quick to*

> *listen, slow to speak and slow to become angry, for man's anger does not bring about the righteous life that God desires* (James 1:19–20).

Results of various communication studies indicate that communication has three main components. Only about seven percent are our *words*, our *tone of voice* accounts for about thirty-eight percent and nearly fifty-five percent is *body language*. So what the listener really hears greatly depends on how we say our words.

- Initiate a meeting to discuss the conflict after emotions are calm. The conflict will not resolve itself. If emotions flare up, stop. Postpone the meeting and seek a solution in your prayer time.
- Often, an uninvolved third party can see the conflict in a different light, and propose reasonable solutions.

4. Give to the one who asks you; do not resist.

> *But I tell you, Do not resist an evil person. If someone strikes you on the right cheek, turn to him the other also. And if someone wants to sue you and take your tunic, let him have your cloak as well. If someone forces you to go one mile, go with him two miles. Give to the one who asks you, and do not turn away from the one who wants to borrow from you* (Matthew 5: 39–42).

Please understand that Jesus is not interested in having disciples who are weak and afraid. He is interested in His disciples valuing people and expressing love.

> *Do nothing out of selfish ambition or vain conceit, but in humility consider others better than yourselves. Each of you should look*

*not only to your own interests, but also to the interests of others* (Philippians 2:3–4).

Giving always maintains and enhances relationships.

5. Prayer is a necessary ingredient.

Retreat from attacking or blaming the one with whom you have conflict, and advance in prayer and in using God's Word against your adversary.

As you pray, you will start to see the conflict in a different light. Pastor Dino Rizzo, Senior Pastor at Healing Place Church, Baton Rouge, Louisiana, says, "My whole world looks totally different when I am on my knees in prayer. Prayer gives me a different perspective."

Those things that seem so important to us in the natural look very different when we spend time in the presence of God.

Pray! Pray together and for each other. Pray before you discuss the issue. Pray, asking God to show you His solution for each issue.

If you disagree with a decision your spouse has made, do not become angry, show disrespect or put them down. We all make mistakes. Love them anyway. Do not allow the decision to drive a wedge between you and your spouse.

6. Agree to disagree.

There are times when, after extended discussions on an issue, no adequate resolution is found. At that point, we just need to agree to disagree and let it go. Let go, for the sake of your relationship.

7. Regain respect.

Have you already lost respect for your spouse or your new child? Pray through! Ask God to re-establish respect in your heart. Make a list of the good qualities that your spouse or each new child has.

8. Admit when you are wrong.

9. Apologize.

Saying “I’m sorry” is mandatory when you have made a mistake or acted poorly.

10. Forgive others for any harsh words spoken, or offensive behavior.

11. Affirm your love and respect for your spouse and family.

# Recommended Resources

## Ministries

**AMFM** *(Association of Marriage and Family Ministry)*
Resources for the marketplace; serving pastors, teachers, trainers, mentors, life coaches, and counselors.
Founders: Eric and Jennifer Garcia
Web site: www.amfmonline.com

**Blending A Family Ministry**
Resources for pre-remarried couples, remarried families, and children of divorce.
Email: blendingafamily@eatel.net or info@blendingafamily.com
Web site: www.blendingafamily.com

**Changing Families**
Making a difference for kids by making it work for their parents.
Tom and Helen Wheeler
Web site: www.changingfamilies.com
Telephone: 843-224-1781

**Divorce Care for Kids** *(DC4K)*
Help your children 5 to 12 years old heal from the pain of divorce.
Linda Jacobs
Web site: www.dc4k.org
Telephone: 1-800-489-7778

**Doing Whatever it Takes**
Resource to help churches and Blended Families connect.
Dr. Shane Stutzman
Web site: www.doingwhateverittakes.org

**Growing Kids God's Way by Growing Families International**
A biblical approach to parenting children.
Greg and Ann Marie Ezzo
Web site: www.gfi.org
Telephone: 319-752-5550

**Interpersonal Communication Programs, Inc.**
Collaborative marriage skills.
Web site: www.couplecommunication.com

**National Center for Biblical Parenting**
Biblical parenting resources.
Dr. Scott Turansky and Joann Miller
Web site: www.biblicalparenting.org
Telephone: 1-800-771-8834

## Reading for Relationships, Marriage and Parenting

*God Breathes on Blended Families Workbook*
by Moe and Paige Becnel

*Love and Respect* (book, DVD, and Small Group Guide)
by Rev. Emerson Eggerichs PhD, www.loveandrespect.com

*Kid CEO—How to keep your children from running your life*
by Ed Young, Pastor, Fellowship Church; Dallas, Texas

*Boundaries—When to Say Yes When to Say No to Take Control of Your Life* (paperback) by Henry Cloud and Dr. John Townsend (Also, *Boundaries Workbook*)

*Saving Your Marriage Before It Starts: Seven Questions to Ask Before and After You Marry* by Les and Leslie Parrott

*The Anger Workbook: A 13-step interactive plan to help you . . .*
by Les Carter, Ph.D. and Frank Minirth, M.D.

*30 Days to Taming Your Tongue: What You Say (and Don't Say) Will Improve Your Relationships* by Deborah Smith Pegues

*Parenting is Heart Work* by Dr. Scott Turansky and Joann Miller

*Growing Kids God's Way; Reaching the Heart of Your Child with a God-Centered Purpose* by Gary and Anne Marie Ezzo

*The Love Dare* by Stephen Kendrick and Alex Kendrick
Visit www.thelovedarebook.com

*Does your Church CONNECT with Blended Families?*
by Dr. Shane Stutzman, www.doingwhateverittakes.org

*Good to Great* by Jim Collins

*Strong Men in Tough Times* by Edwin Louis Cole

*Maximized Manhood: A Guide to Family Survival* by Edwin Louis Cole

*The Unique Woman* by Edwin Louis Cole and Nancy Corbett Cole

*Expectation* by Dr. Mike Brown, www.stronginthelord.org

## Reading for Singles

*Dating with Pure Passion: More than Rules, More than Courtship, More than a Formula* by Rob Eagar

*The Ten Commandments of Dating: Time-Tested Laws for Building Successful Relationships* by Ben Young and Samuel Adams

*I Kissed Dating Goodbye* by Joshua Harris

# About Blending A Family Ministry

## *Mission Statement*

*The mission of Blending A Family Ministry is to be a healing place, to be a source of hope and help for today's remarried families, to give guidance concerning the issues that Blended Families face, to help remarried couples and their children to become the very best family that God intended, to dismiss the thought that Blended Families are second class families, and to see thousands of Blended Families flourish as they develop into the loving, peace-filled safe-haven that God intended the home to be.*

▪ ▪ ▪

BLENDING A FAMILY MINISTRY (BAF) was founded in 2002 to be a resource for Blended Families that desire God's plan and God's best for their families.

Our goal is to help blended families become loving families, and to see these families overcome life's issues and *thrive*, not just survive. The Blended Family needs to provide a solid foundation for its children, established through God's love, mercy, grace, and principles. The desired result is for the cycle of divorce to be broken in couples' lives, and in their children's lives.

BAF has developed materials that have proven to be a source of hope, encouragement and guidance as people see that what the Becnels experienced in their family is similar to what many other Blended Families face.

Their first book, *God Breathes on Blended Families* (first edition 2000), is a testimony of the Becnel family becoming a loving family. The book was written to give hope and guidance to all Blended Families that they, too, can become true loving families.

The second edition (2009), which you now hold in your hands, contains nine additional years of knowledge and experience. *God Breathes on Blended Families Workbook* was written to assist couples in applying the principles discussed in *God Breathes on Blended Families* to their own families. God has truly blessed this work, using it to help other families find success. The authors have seen and heard many positive results from families who have read and applied the fundamentals presented in the book.

Many churches are using the *God Breathes on Blended Families* book and workbook together to teach a Blended Family Support Group.

*Blending A Family Ministry promotes . . .*

- receiving and living in God's forgiveness when we repent and turn from our self-pleasing lifestyles,
- building strong marriages and healthy, peace-filled, loving families that last a lifetime,
- the new Blended Family being the source of healing from past hurts for the children involved, and
- breaking the cycle of divorce in people's lives and in the lives of their children.

*Become a Blending A Family Support Group leader in your church or community.*

Contact us for more information.

Email: blendingafamily@eatel.net
info@blendingafamily.com

Web site: www.blendingafamily.com

# About the Authors

MOE AND PAIGE BECNEL are natives of New Orleans, Louisiana, and reside in Baton Rouge with their dog, Belle. They met in 1987 and married in 1989, blending a family of five children.

Formerly in the utility business, medical field, and Singles Pastors at Healing Place Church in Baton Rouge, (leading singles, single parent, divorce recovery and Blended Family ministries), the Becnels founded Blending A Family Ministry in 2002. The Becnels are available for:

- Blended Family Seminars
- marriage seminars and conferences
- discussion groups
- singles conferences
- individual Blended Family guidance

### *Contact the Authors*

To set up speaking engagements, or for personal assistance:

Email: blendingafamily@eatel.net
info@blendingafamily.com

Web site: www.blendingafamily.com

notes:

notes:

notes:

notes:

notes: